THE AUTOBIOGRAPHY OF CLABON JONES

THE AUTOBIOGRAPHY OF CLABON JONES

*The Clabon Jones Experience in the Bayou
Country of Louisiana and in Vietnam*

CLABON JONES

authorHOUSE®

AuthorHouse™ LLC
1663 Liberty Drive
Bloomington, IN 47403
www.authorhouse.com
Phone: 1-800-839-8640

Published by AuthorHouse   12/13/2013

ISBN: 978-1-4918-3656-9 (sc)
ISBN: 978-1-4918-3658-3 (hc)
ISBN: 978-1-4918-3655-2 (e)

Library of Congress Control Number: 2013920700

CONTENTS

CONTENTS

ACKNOWLEDGMENTS

Having already thanked God and continuing to do so, I also want to thank this country for taking care of me when I came back disabled even though I did have some problems making the government do what it was supposed to do. Nonetheless, this country does recognize its veteran and treats us with some degree of respect. We do have Veterans' Day, Memorial Day and such, and most veterans get benefits even though some are not getting the benefits that they are entitled to. Hence, we veterans are blessed because we are living in a country where the federal government helps us financially, in recognition of what we did for the United States. There are, unfortunately other countries that do not take care of their men after they have fought and suffered in wars for them.

Additionally, I want to give special thanks to my wife, Patricia G. Jones. I want to thank her for being a wonderful support to me.

Last, but by no means least, I want to give special homage, special roots, I will call it, to my parents—Roland and Lillian Jones. They are gone but not forgotten. Their teaching and training were a big part of what has guided me through the years. Specifically, my father's love and understanding of me allowed me to be me (always curious, always questioning and always getting in and out of trouble). His faith in me, his realizing that I was inquisitive and rambunctious but not bad, empowered me to believe in myself so much until nothing could break my spirit. I emphatically say, "Thank you, Mother and Father, for all that you did. May you rest in peace!"

Now to the readers, those of you who have honored me by buying this book, I hope and pray that it will be meaningful to you. I hope that whenever you are feeling down and out or you think that you are the only person going through rough times, you will pick this book up and read it. Hopefully, you will see that you are not the only one who has had hard times. Prayerfully, you will see that the mighty God who took care of a little precocious black boy from the Louisiana bayous, saw him safely through early manhood in the Vietnam jungles and who continues to sustain him daily, is the same God who has His eyes and hands on you.

May God bless you, and I sincerely thank you!

THE CHILDHOOD YEARS

I was conceived on a plantation in Lakeland, Louisiana, two miles from Oscar, where I was born on July 5, 1949 at 1:20 A.M., almost half a century ago. Indeed, I was born in Oscar, a little country community on False River, six miles from New Roads, which is about thirty miles from Baton Rouge, the capitol.

I take pride in having been born in Oscar since that is where my parents fled in their attempt to better themselves when they left the plantation where my grandmother, Edna Jones Rowan, lived. My parents fled to Oscar for what they considered to be a better life, and Oscar is where bittersweet life began.

My family lived in a three-room shotgun house on the field side of Oscar, where the majority of the black folk lived. Most of the white folk lived in nice, spacious plantation-style homes on the riverside of Oscar.

And so, it was the water, the river and the bayou, which served as the natural barriers that separated the races, the blacks from the white, and that separated those who had from those who had not.

Even though my family was part of the had nots, and we were poor, impoverished people, I did not know it at the time and was happy in my modest childhood there in Oscar, Louisiana.

According to my mother, I was a fat and happy baby who literally stayed a baby until I was three years old and finally decided to walk. It seems that I was content emulating my wheelchair-bound sister who was

1

paralyzed from the chest down, and I refused to walk until I felt good and ready to do so, shortly after my third birthday. The report my mother gave was that I bypassed crawling, stumbling, and toddling, and started to actually walk in one day's time. It appears that my mother discovered me standing on my feet when she came inside from hanging clothes on the clothesline. I walked towards her and kept walking from that day forth. In fact, the story goes that I started to walk that day and have been hard to keep up with every since.

I do not remember that eventful day when I was three back in 1952, but I do recall other things that were going on in my life around that time. I remember being too young to work in the fields as my parents and older siblings did. So, I spent my time playing. I played in the fields, in the corn crib, tumbling amongst the corn and the potatoes. I also played in the front yard, on the soft, green grass that my father kept cut with a handheld swing blade. I remember that the grass was always cut low so that we kids could play in it and so that snakes could not hide in it.

At three and four years of age, my job was playing, and that is what I did well. I played alone and with my brothers and sisters because we could not play with other kids in the neighborhood. My parents did not allow us to play with those "messy" kids who were quick to taunt us, call us names and fight us.

Because my parents were strict and had specific rules and regulations about what we could and could not do or where we could and could not go, many of the black folk and their kids thought that we were trying to be "uppity," and even called us "Big Shit." The fact that we had straight "fair" hair and light brown complexions, did not help either. So, my siblings and I had trouble at home in the neighborhood, and later on when we went to school. The black kids from the country would often tell the city kids in town to jump on us Jones kids and beat us up, and the city kids, being afraid of the big, cornbread-fed country kids, would fight us on command for fear of having their own butts whipped. Thus, we not only had to contend with prejudice from the whites, but from our fellow "messy" blacks, as wells.

Nevertheless, life was not all bad. In fact, I can recall many good times during my early childhood. I particularly enjoyed the times when Uncle Jesse would visit us.

Uncle Jesse was from New Orleans, and he had that cool, smooth, New Orleans style about him. He would come to Oscar clean! He would be decked out in his heavily starched and creased khakis, white shirt and spit-shined black shoes, with white socks, and a red handkerchief draping from his left back pocket. As a child, I was really impressed by the way Uncle Jesse carried himself, and as an adult, I still admire the style and finesse he showed as a black man during that time.

Uncle Jesse would pull into our yard in his big, brown Ford loaded with all kinds of goodies for his brother Roland, my father, and our family. He would have that Ford packed with shoes, clothes, watermelons, grapes, cantaloupes, bananas, and all kinds of fruit. We were always excited about all of the stuff Uncle Jesse brought. The immediate family and the extended family of my aunts and uncles usually knew of Uncle Jesse's expected visit, so when he arrived, unloaded the car and settled in, the good times would begin.

Miss. Ruth, Uncle Jesse's wife, and mama would start a fire in the old wooden stove in the kitchen and commence to cooking. They would have a ball talking and catching up on the family news and gossip. Uncle Jesse, my daddy, and my other uncles would sit on the front porch, rolling cigarettes, talking, laughing and having fun. We kids would be out in the front yard, shooting marbles, swinging on the tree swing, playing with our slingshots or spinning tops, waiting for the fresh baked yeast bread that mama would give us, along with some canned peaches, pears or figs, to snack on while the "real food" was being prepared.

Speaking of the freshly baked bread reminds me of the butt whippings I got causing the yeast bread to fall when I ran or walked too hard across the rickety wooden floors in our house while the yeast was rising. Boy! It was dangerous walking across mama's floor while bread was in the making.

By the time the "real food" got ready, there would be a big crowd gathered at our house; a crowd of aunts and uncles who were smoking, drinking, and having a good time. Mama and Miss. Ruth would lay the spread out on the table, and it was clear to anybody with eyes that we were not short on food. The meal usually included mustard, turnip, or collard greens, chitlings, fried chicken, sweet potatoes, crawfish etoufee, seafood gumbo, dirty rice, boudin, hoghead cheese, crawfish bisque, okra gumbo, bread pudding, and other Louisiana Creole and Cajun dishes.

Most of what we ate was what we raised or grew. There was not a lot of store-bought stuff on our tables. Granted, we were poor, but we always had plenty of food that we did not mind sharing with kinfolk on special occasions like Uncle Jesse's visits.

Yes, one or two hogs were killed, and a cow was butchered every fall, and every fall my father would share the meat with everyone in the community, even his enemies. The fall butchering ensured that we would always have lots of meat to go along with the fruits and vegetables mama canned in the summertime so that the family could eat well the whole year. We would get peas, green beans, cabbage, onions, okra, tomatoes, peaches, pears, figs, and other fresh produce from the garden during the spring and summer, and have a well stocked pantry of these canned foods for the winter. So, Thanksgiving, Christmas, Uncle Jesse's visits, or any celebration, simply gave us a good reason to get together, eat, and have a great time enjoying the fruits, vegetables, and meats of our labor.

In 1954, when I turned five years old, my carefree childhood of doing nothing but playing came to a screeching halt. By the time my fifth birthday rolled around, my parents had decided that I needed to do something besides get into mischief around the house. Hence, I was introduced to the world of work. Manual work; hard, gritty, grinding work that was far from child's play.

Around the first of March of my fifth year on earth, when it was time for my daddy to start plowing fields and bursting water dreans, getting ready to plant corn, cotton and cane, I became the official water boy. It is ironic that my father had the same job back in 1913, when he was five years old.

As a water boy, I hauled gallons of jugs of water to the fields, walking on the scorching ground with my bare feet, fighting the hot sun, dodging snakes, and struggling to survive. As I think back now, at age five, I was doing to a lesser degree some of the same stuff I was doing at age eighteen in the fields of Vietnam, but I'll talk more about that later.

I was the water boy as my daddy sharecropped on Mr. Earnest Bourdeaux's farm. My daddy's job was to plant and harvest Mr. Bourdeaux's crops for a share of the profits, and he did not have a problem with that since that was the way most black folk made their living during that time. In fact, sharecropping was considered a step up on the economic ladder during those days.

What caused a problem for my daddy was that Mr. Bourdeaux, and apparently every other white man in Oscar, expected him to continue working the crops with a sideboard and mule, while white farmers used tractors. My daddy was turned down time and time again when he approached bankers, trying to borrow money to purchase a tractor. When he stood up and absolutely refused to work the fields any longer without a tractor, Mr. Bourdeaux gave in and purchased one, and my daddy ended up with a brand new, Alice Chandler tractor to use to farm the land for his and Mr. Bourdeaux's crops.

And so it was! My daddy sharecropped year after year, and I was the water boy, learning how to run zigzag through the fields to outrun the Blue Runner Snakes as I brought water to my parents and siblings while they chopped cotton, corn, and cane. When I grew older, I graduated from water boy to one of the field hands who chopped, picked, and pulled the crops along with everybody else.

In addition to working in the fields, we also picked pecans. When the pecans did not bear and fall fast enough, we would climb into the trees and thrash them (beat the limbs) so that the pecans would fall to the ground and we could pick them. When there were few pecans, the rats would have to go on welfare because we would rob the pecans that they had stored in their nests for the winter. That way, we had pecans to sell even when the pecans were not plentiful. In those situations, we were the ones who had, and rats were the ones who had not.

As I grew older, I continued to work in the fields and at Mr. Bourdeaux's house, straightening up and doing whatever chores I was asked to do. Oftentimes, as I was walking on my way to his house to work, Mr. Bourdeaux would drive by and give me a ride in his truck. His trucks were always nice and roomy, and it seemed to me that he got a new one every year.

While I rode in Mr. Bourdeaux's vehicle, I would be thinking and wondering to myself why it was that Mr. Bourdeaux had such a nice, big truck to ride around in, while my daddy and the rest of us had to walk everywhere we went. As I worked around Mr. Bourdeaux's house, cutting grass, feeding his chickens, cows and hogs, I would frequently get a chance to go inside to do some chores that he had for me, and I would marvel at the beauty of his home, a huge structure elegantly filled with lovely furniture. I would get a glimpse of his closet, jam-packed with clothes and shoes, and his wife's closet would be the same way. There would be all kinds of jewelry lying out on their dresser and dangling from the armoire. The house was loaded with all kinds of fine trappings, indicative of their great wealth. I would go from room to room in their big house, and I would often catch myself looking out of their clear, bright windows, and I would see the three-room shanty where my mama, my daddy, my nine brothers and sisters and I lived, just a hop, skip and jump from Mr. Bourdeaux's domicile.

Even as a child, I could see the difference in our lifestyles and wondered why the white folk had so much, while the black folk had so little. I was a child, less than twelve years and not even at the age of accountability yet, but I could plainly see that people's accounts in life were not even and balanced.

And so, at nine, ten, and eleven years old, I knew that there had to be something else. Something better for black folk than being treated like herds of cattle, being driven to death working as sharecroppers for just a little, tiny share of the crop. I knew that there had to be better ways of making a living than getting $3.50 for 100 pounds of cotton. I knew there was something wrong with Mr. Bourdeaux having fifteen pairs of shoes, and my daddy having only two pairs—one pair to work in, and one pair for church, and sometimes having only one pair that served both purposes.

So, usually when I finished working at Mr. Bourdeaux's house and was on my way home, I left the premise feeling dejected, with my head hung down, my hands in my pocket, and my mind deep in thought, trying to figure out what was wrong with the picture I saw when I looked at what Mr. Bourdeaux had and what we had, especially in view of who did the real work. Yes, my child's mind was always busy making comparisons, juxtaposing Mr. Bourdeaux's mansion filled with luxurious furnishings to our three-room hut with a bed in the front room, a bed in the middle room, and a wood cook stove in the tiny kitchen where gnats, flies, and even birds few in whenever they felt like it, through a small wooden door that served as a window. In Mr. Bourdeaux's house, crystal chandeliers hung from the ceiling. In my house, snakes hung from the ceiling on more than one occasion.

I recall one specific incident that my mother told me about. She said that one day when I was a baby, she came into the house from being outside at the clothes line, and there was this big, long, black snake hanging from the loft directly over me as I lay on the bed. She ran out of the house screaming and scared to death. She ran to the field where my daddy was plowing, told him about the snake, and fearfully followed him back to the house. He bravely went inside, killed the snake, then went back to the field and continued plowing as if nothing unusual had happened.

Stories such as this merely emphasized to me the great difference between what we had and how we lived, and what Mr. Bourdeaux had and how he lived. This all confused me when I was a child; all of this troubled me then, and it still troubles me now.

One of my favorite pastimes when I was a younger boy, around the age of ten or eleven, was going down to the river. Often I would ask my parents if I could go down to False River. I would not have dared to go without permission because the river was considered very dangerous since several kids had drowned in it, and parents were cautious about their kids being there.

Usually my parents would let me go and I would go down there and play with my white friends, Tooter and Johnny. When I played with them, I would go into their place which was called The Lighthouse. It was a little café there on the river. I could go inside The Lighthouse if I were working in there with Tooter and Johnny or if I were putting drinks in the drink machine to fill it up. However, after we had played all morning and it was time for lunch, I could not eat inside The Lighthouse; I had to eat on the back porch. Of course, Tooter and Johnny would eat their lunch inside.

When my parents found out about the eating arrangements, they hit the roof! My mother marched down to The Lighthouse and told Tooter's mother, Miss. Nina, strict and straight and if I were going to play with Tooter, then I could very well eat with him, too. She said that if it happened again, I definitely could not play with Tooter. She told Miss.

Nina that when Tooter played at my house, she made him welcome to whatever she cooked, and he and I always ate together, whether it was outside under the tree or on the front porch, it was together! She went on to tell Miss. Nina that if she heard of me eating on the back porch again, she was not only going to not let me play with Tooter, she was going to come down there and "tear her ass up" about it. Mr. Nina heard what mama said and tried to get smart-mouthed with mama, but mama was ready to jump on him, too. She was just that bold, and would have fought a man as quickly as she would a woman. Back then, a black woman fighting with a white man was nothing strange. Believe me! If people think that black women are strong now, they should have seen my mama. In those days, she would have fought an elephant.

I can also recall when I used to go to the fields to play by myself. The back fields were no distance from my house, and my house was surrounded by white folk's houses. The Augillards lived behind us; the Duprees lived beside us; the Gremillions lived on one side of us and Mr. Lebo and his wife, Lucille, and his son TeeJack (yes, his name was TeeJack, believe it or not) lived on the other side of us. That put our house right in the middle of all the white folk's houses.

Well, one day I walked to the back to the fields, and I saw the strangest thing! There was a meeting going on right there in the fields. There was this big group of men, and they were burning crosses and talking. I walked right dead into the middle of them, little of me, an innocent kid, just a boy, not knowing anything. I heard one of the men say, "Oh, that's Roland's boy!"

Now, they knew my daddy, and they knew that he did not play; he was not scary; and he would not take any mess from anybody. They knew that if anything happened to any of his children, my daddy would come after them with his double-barreled shotgun, and a bunch of other black folk would come after them, too, which just goes to show how we blacks might fight each other, but when it comes to stuff like that, we blacks come together.

The bottom line is that the clansmen did not bother me. I walked straight through their meeting unharmed, but confused. I was a puzzled child trying to figure out what was going on. I was thinking that those people were trying to baptize each other by fire. I knew that blacks baptized each other in the water at the river. As I walked away from the group, I looked back and was thinking that was the strangest thing. I heard them talking, saying, "nigger this," and, "nigger that," and, "let's kill the niggers!" but to me, at the time, all of this meant nothing because I was a child.

So, there I was again, walking home with my head down, my hands in my pockets, kicking the dust and trying to figure stuff out! When I got home, I said to my daddy, "Daddy, you know, it's the strangest thing. I saw these white people back in the fields baptizing each other by fire. Don't we baptize in the river? They've got a strange way of baptizing!" My daddy simply said, "Boy, don't every pay those people any mind. Those people are crazy; they don't have good sense. They are some real ignorant people. You stay out of their company. Next time you see them gathered up like that, you either go in the cotton patch or in the cane patch. Don't go around them." I said, "They didn't do me nothing." He then asked, "Where did you go?" I replied, "I just walked right in the middle of them." He asked, "None of them bothered you?" I answered, "No sir! They didn't do me nothing." And I asked again, "Why don't they go to the river to get baptized?"

My daddy did not explain that I had just walked through a Ku Klux Klan meeting. He did not tell me anything about what the Ku Klux Klan was, but as I grew up, I started to hear more and more about the KKK, and I learned what they were all about.

Yet, the ironic thing was that I played with clansmen's daughters. Their daughters would come to my house, Bobby Kay, Mattis, and

Meggy, all of them. They would come by and we would play. We would throw dirt, wallow and wrestle with each other. Yes, I mean the girls; the girls and boys, all of us, my brothers and sisters. We all played with each other, it was a stupid thing.

Still another incident is deeply buried in my memory, also. One evening, my parents were sitting on the front porch. We kids were out in the yard playing. An old tire was burning so that its smoke would ward off mosquitoes. I looked up and saw the clansmen coming out of their houses with their suits on, the white sheets with mouth and eye holes in them that they wore to hide who they were. They waved and spoke to my daddy on their way to the city, to the town to disturb the peace by harassing the black folk in New Roads and Baton Rouge. They were not about to mess with my daddy because he had a record of kicking behinds. They passed us at our house and went on to New Roads and Baton Rouge and raised cain with the black folk in those towns. Then, later that night, we heard them coming back to their houses, and the next day they were back out in the fields with us like we were all best friends.

Being a kid, I did not know. I did not know about prejudice. There were no slang words thrown around in my house; we were not allowed to call white people names. My parents did not teach us to call them nicknames or anything like that. But, the smallest white kid would come around and call us nigger this and nigger that. Eventually, as we were growing up, my parents taught us that their calling us nigger showed how much they did not like us. So, we kids soon learned, and as soon as somebody called me a nigger, I was ready to pop the hell out of him. I would pop the first kid to call me a nigger, give him a black eye or whatever. But the strangest thing was that within an hour or so, I would be playing with the same kid that I had popped for calling me a nigger, because that is how things were with us kids.

Sometimes, their parents would come over to our house about an incident that had happened, but my parents had a way of handling things. They knew white folk; they lived in the middle of them, and somehow things always got smoothed out.

What was amazing was that the white neighbors thought that they knew us. Every time the white neighbors needed a hand getting their crops in or needed help pulling their corn, they acted like my daddy's children were a gang of slaves for them. Before the harvest started, they would come by or talk to my daddy over the fence, petting him up because they knew the cotton was getting ready to be picked, the corn was getting ready to die, and everything was ready for harvest. They would bring corn over to my daddy when it first got ripe, trying to get on his good side. Daddy had his own corn, but he would take theirs just to go along with them. Yet, he knew the game they were playing, and he knew that they were the ones on the ignorant side, because he knew them far better than they knew him. He knew that when they came to the house for their so-called friendly smoke and conversation, what they really came over for was to solicit his help in gathering their crops. And we all knew what the conversation between my daddy and the white neighbor was about. We knew simply by seeing them walking out into the fields, looking at the crops. As the crops grew, the white folk got friendlier and friendlier.

The same thing would happen when they ran for political office and wanted black people's votes. All they did was have a big picnic, and I am sorry to say, there would be one sorry, Uncle Tom-type black man that would encourage the blacks to come out and support the white candidate. The white candidate would have a big shindig with a free beer bus, plenty of free food, free this and free that.

However, my daddy never fell for any of that. My parents were smart people and were not fooled by the white man's political hogwash. They knew that as soon as the white candidates got elected, they would start paving the roads and digging the ditches out in the white areas, which they are still doing today. They knew that the white elected officials were not going to try and improve the black neighborhoods.

Even though my daddy never participated in their free food rallies and such, there were always whites around who thought that they were smart; they always thought that we blacks were ignorant and stupid, and they were smarter and better than us. So, my daddy had to show them who was smarter; he showed them in his clever own way. When harvest time came, grinding time as we called, my daddy would not let any of us go pick their cotton, pull their corn or chop their cane. We helped no one except for the owner of the place where we lived, Mr. Earnest Bourdeaux. We had to harvest his crops, and my daddy did make a share off those crops; that is why he was called a sharecropper. In other words, my daddy did all the work, but the white man got the big money.

Under those circumstances, my daddy could not progress as fast as he wanted to; he was still in a slavery-type situation. The housing on the place was inadequate, and the landowner would not make needed repairs. When it rained, the roof leaked, and there would be ninety pots set on the floor to catch the rain. Then, as soon as the rain stopped, we had to crawl on top of the house to put tar on the roof and try to stop the leak.

Nevertheless, my daddy—my parents—did the best they could do with what they had; they did the best they could with the little education that they had. And the main thing was that my parents prayed; people in general prayed back then during those hard times. We always had prayer in our home, and the white folk were thinking evil, we were busy praying.

As I think back now, I believe that we lived a better, healthier, a more prosperous life than they did, even though they had all the money and the beautiful homes, the warm and cool homes—the warm homes in the winter, and cool homes in the summertime.

One thing was for sure, our lives were full and rich with activities. I cannot remember ever being truly bored, particularly since I was what was known now as a precocious child, full of energy and curious. I was the kind of child that, if I were told not to walk into the fire because it would burn me, I would go ahead and try it anyway. I was the type of kid that wanted to know "why" about everything. Since the moon and stars were in the sky, I wanted to know how they got there. I wanted to know why I could not do this, or could not do that. Even if I were told or shown something and told that it was dangerous and I should not try it, I would always do the opposite of what I was told to see if I could master it for myself. Consequently, I was always getting into something, or finding myself in the middle of something. Like the situation with the henhouse.

My daddy knew that I liked to go into the henhouse to get the eggs from underneath the hens, which the hens did not appreciate because they were sitting on the eggs to try to hatch them. I had been pecked by an annoyed hen once, and my daddy told me stay out of the henhouse, because not only did the hens not like me messing with their eggs, there were snakes in there, too, looking for eggs. Needless to say, one day while mama was busy cleaning up and washing clothes, and the kids were playing in the yard, I sneaked back to the henhouse. There were a few chickens in there, but most of the chickens were outside, pecking around on the ground for worms and other food. There was this one, big, black and white speckled hen sitting on her eggs. Her nest was right at my eye level, so, when I stuck my hands under her to get eggs, she quickly pecked me dead in the eye. I broke away and started running, screaming, crying, and holding my eye. I ran into the door of the henhouse, which knocked me to the ground. I wallowed and moaned on the ground, got up, and ran out hollering. My mother came out, grabbed me, and saw where the hen had pecked me in the eye. I was still hollering and crying, and she was steadily trying to calm me down. Finally, she was able to quiet me down and calm her nerves, also. That is when she asked, "Boy, what were you doing in the henhouse? Did Sun (her nickname for my daddy because his complexion was light and red like the sun) tell you to stay out of the henhouse?" I said, "Yeah!" She yelled, "Boy, I'll kill you!"

I said, "I'm almost dead now!" She broke a branch off a tree and started whipping me. I forgot about my eye as she was beating me. I broke loose from her and ran straight under the house to my refuge where I knew I would be safe, because my mama could not run under the house after me.

However, there was one drawback to running under the house. Later, it got dark, and I had to come from under the house and go inside. Nevertheless, it was my refuge, and I stayed under the house to let things cool down. During this particular day, I stayed a little while and listened to my mama complaining about what I had done. She eventually stopped saying anything, and I felt that it was safe to come out from under the house. For whatever reason, my mother seemed more forgiving than my daddy. She would beat my butt, do what she had to do, and soon forget about it. Daddy, on the other hand, did not forget and forgive right then and there. It took him a while.

Later that evening, as I had come from under the house and was playing in the backyard, my daddy came home from working in the fields and sat on the back steps, rolling his cigarette. He saw me and my bloodshot eye and asked, "Boy, what happened?" I answered, "Nothing!" He yelled to my mother, "Lizzie, what happened to that boy's eye?" Mama replied with, "Oh yes, I forgot to tell you what that boy did!" Man! When she said that, I broke to run, but my daddy caught me by my collar because he knew I had gotten into something. He got the full story from my mama, and by the time he did, he had dragged me to a tree and broken off a limb with his big hands that looked like a backhoe. He did not wiggle or struggle to break the limb off; he snapped it off with one snap and started wearing me out. I was hollering, screaming and trying to get loose. My trick was to run between his legs so that I could take my foot and push against one of his feet to get loose. When I got loose, I ran straight under the house. However, the bad thing was that it was getting dark, and I knew I had to face the blues and go inside. What I decided to do was wait it out. I knew that if I let my daddy get a little rest and have a little time with my mama to discuss business and such, then he would be in a more passive mood and less likely to want to whip me for what I had done. So, I let him get his coffee and his conversation started with mama, and then I slowly crept from under the house, making a little noise to let them hear me. When my daddy said, "Boy, I see you, I hope you aren't trying to make fun with me," I knew he had calmed down, and I was not going to get another whipping that night. My calculation was that he was tired. I always noticed my parents carefully, and I noticed that when they had time to rest, drink some coffee, and talk, they were usually in a better mood.

As I said previously, I was a curious child, but I was an observant child, as well. I was always watching my parents and others, and usually someone was watching me, too. Like the day I got bit in the eye by our dog, Rex.

On this particular day, my brother was up in our tree house, eating some chicken. I wanted a piece, so he threw a piece down to me. Well, the dog jumped for the chicken at the same time that I went up for it, and the dog accidentally bit me over my eye. Boy, it hurt something awful! I started crying; I was really crying. My daddy came, looked at my eye, and got really worked up about it. He yelled for my mother to bring a piece of fat meat to put on my eye to reduce the swelling and to help the cut heal faster.

I was hurting, but I knew that the dog did not mean any harm. He was just trying to catch the chicken; the chicken came too close to my face, and he bit me. However, this did not matter to my father. After a while, when things had calmed down, my daddy took his shotgun, walked the dog to the back of the field while we all just sat looking at him. In a few minutes, all we heard was, "room, room," the muffled sounds of a fatally wounded dog. My daddy killed the dog, and I said, "There goes poor Rex. Poor Rex got killed behind me when I should have left the food alone."

Even though my parents had their problems with all of us, I was more aggressive than my siblings, so my parents always kept an eye on me. I recall the time when it was the first of the year and my daddy had gone to New Orleans to find work with my Uncle Jesse. We were all around the house, outside playing. My brothers were in the yard shooting marbles; my sisters were playing house, making tea cakes and mud pies out of dirt. I was restless, sitting on the front porch steps. I wanted to go and play with Peter and Paul and the other boys, but my mama said no, that I was not to leave the front yard. I did not say anything to her, I knew better than to argue or talk back, because that would have been a sure butt beating. So, I sat there on the steps with my mouth poked out, pouting. Then, I looked back at the house at the screen door; I could not see mama. I saw Paul walking by over on the road, and that really gave me the urge to go. I said to myself, "man, I can't sit on this porch all day; I've got to go play with the rest of the kids." I got up off the porch and started toward the gate. My brothers were watching me very keenly, because they knew that I would get into something pretty quick! I did not see mama through the screen door, but she saw me and yelled, "Didn't I tell you not to go outside this yard?" She came out onto the porch with her gun, pointed that gun at me and screamed, "Come back here!" I cried out, "Mama, don't shoot me!" I was getting ready to go out of the gate and I looked around and looked dead into that double-barreled shotgun. She yelled again, "Come back here! Didn't I tell you not to go outside this yard?" I said, "Yes, ma'am!" "Where are you going?" she asked again. I said, "Nowhere!" She yelled, "You're lying! Don't you know I'm going to kill you?" I held my hand out and screamed, "Oh, no! Please don't shoot me!" She was holding the gun in my face and I was crying and crying. I was crying so much, but while I was crying, I was also looking around. I looked over to my right side and saw that old black Plymouth that was parked in the front yard. It was old and broken down, but it would run when we gave it a push. Anyway, it was parked there in our front yard, and I thought for sure that mama was going to shoot me. So, I ran and slid under the old Plymouth. It was low to the ground, but not as low as the cars are today, and I could not run under the car like I used to run when I hid under the house. Mama came to the car, stooped down, pointed that shotgun in my face and said, "If you don't come from under this car, I'm going to pull the trigger!" Now, picture me, as a child, looking down the barrel of this double-barreled shotgun. Of course, the gun was not loaded, and she was only using it to scare me, to make me come out so that she could get hands on me to wear my behind out. She said, "I'm giving you three seconds to come out from under there!" I said, "Okay, I'm not going to do it anymore!" She said, "Come to me, come to me!" As soon as I came out, she dropped the gun, and man, she started in on me! She grabbed me in my chest and was hitting me with her right hand, back and forth, back and forth, back handing me and showing no mercy. I was trying hard to get away from her, and finally I did break loose and I ran under the house because that was my little spot, my refuge from my parents whenever I got in trouble.

I was hoping and praying that mama would not tell my daddy about that incident when he got home. Well, that incident was not that crucial because we had been getting into things all day. By the time my daddy got home that evening, she had forgotten about it, and I had nothing to worry about.

However, incidents like these led my oldest brother to give me the nickname Thraka. In Creole, Thraka mean "trouble." I was trouble, sure enough, because I was always listening when my older brothers were planning and plotting about how they were going to leave the house, or about what they were going to do down at the canal where they went fishing. The canal was on False River; it ran from False River, across the road, underneath the road and back down into the fields. Usually they were scheming to meet some young ladies that lived in the area, and I would be listening to every word. They never paid any attention to me because I was young and just a little kid. But, the fact was, I would run and tell my mother. I would say, "Ma Moun (the name I often called her), Junior'em fixin' to leave from here, and they're going to meet some women back in the field." Everything my brothers did got back to my mama, and they wondered how in the world she was finding out. She would find out what they were up to and stop them. As this kept happening, my older brother got mad and he accused my other brother of ratting on them.

On one particular occasion, after mama had interrupted their plans, Temel and Nunu yelled to my brother, "Totee (Totee means turtle in Creole, the name he got because he was red like a red snapping turtle, red and high yellow like my daddy), you must be telling your mama all of our plans." Naturally, Totee said that he had not, and he declared that he did not know how my mother was finding out about everything. He said, "Maybe we need to move farther out in the yard when we talk, out by the gate away from the house." So, they moved out by the gate and started to plot about how they were going to take the field side and walk back to the field as if they were going to the fields to pick pecans, check on the watermelons or eat some persimmons. I, of course, had heard the whole scenario and went straight to my mother and shouted, "Ma Moun, Junior'em ain't going to eat no watermelons or persimmons. They're going to the fields and then to the bayou. They are going to cross the bayou and go on to the road to New Roads to meet some women!" My mother was preoccupied and half listened to me, so I repeated my message, "Ma Moun, I'm telling you! Junior'em ain't going to eat no watermelons or persimmons. They are going to meet some women!" Finally, my mama took heed to what I was saying, and again, she stopped them before their plans materialized. Boy! Junior was mad! He jerked his cap off his head, slapped it across his leg, and shouted, "Got dog! Everything I do, she knows about it!"

Their plotting and mama's finding out went on for some time, and they were steadily trying to figure out how she knew. Finally, they became more watchful and more suspicious, and one particular day they noticed that I was not out playing marbles or spinning toys with the rest of the little kids. They concluded that I was usually hanging around them. That's what Temel and Nunu yelled, "This is the rascal that has been telling everything we do!" When they said that, I looked up at them, and they were tall and towering over me. My eyes got big and I ran screaming, "Mama, mama! Help me! They're going to beat me! They're going to beat me!" And that's how I earned the name Thraka. From that day forth, they knew that if they were planning anything, they had better not let me know about it.

As time passed, and I grew older, I still remained a curious, inquisitive child. Often I would see my daddy coming from the field where he had been bursting water dreans with his mule. He would put the mule in the pasture which was right beside our house, with a fence separating the pasture from the yard.

My daddy always told me not to ever mess with the mule. He would say, "Boy, don't you ever fool around with that mule because he will kick you, and he can hurt you real bad." I would never say anything; I would just look and listen to my daddy. I also noticed how my daddy would put the bridle on the mule; I noticed how he would hitch him up and everything. Well, one Friday afternoon, my daddy came from the field, unhitched the mule, and let him run free in the pasture. When he and the rest of the family were inside the house entertaining the company we had, I decided to hitch the mule up. The bridle was very heavy; it weighed about sixty-five pounds, and I weighed about the same. I was struggling to get the bridle on and the mule hitched up. I was between the mule's leg, bent over, trying my hardest to get the bridle on. Luckily, my father glanced out of the kitchen window as he was getting himself some coffee, and he saw me. There I was, between the mule's legs. The mule was prancing around, and I was struggling. My daddy dashed out of the house, ran to me and the mule, and tried to keep the mule steady while he got me loose. Finally, he got me out, and there I was, in trouble again. My daddy dragged me by my shirt collar to the house. I was trying to get loose, but those big bear hands of his just dragged me on. He took those big hands and snapped a limb from a tree and wore my little behind out! I mean! He whipped me for a lifetime; he whipped me until he got tired. When he turned me loose, I was hurt and shamed, and I made my usual dash straight under the house. Everybody else was fine; all the other kids were laughing and playing and doing what they were supposed to be doing, and my parents went on entertaining their company.

As I said, this incident happened on a Friday. By Sunday, this had all blown over, and my family was preparing for a big party. Everybody was going to be there—my aunts and uncles and cousins and all, plenty of kids. Uncle Jesse had come down from New Orleans. Everything was exciting and I knew we were getting ready to have a good time. So, on Sunday afternoon, everybody started coming by the house. My aunts and their husbands came, and they all started drinking and carrying on. I got ready to have myself some fun.

Everybody was on the front porch eating and having a great time. The kids were out in the yard playing marbles and their usual games. I was out there playing, too, but suddenly, I got bored playing marbles. I decided that playing spinning tops was boring, and I thought that playing in the trees was first grade stuff. I figured that I had to find myself something else to do. I first looked at the car; I had looked at the engines of cars a lot before and tried to figure out how things worked. I looked at the different gauges and gadgets, and I knew that the starter down on the floor of the car and accelerator all worked together to make the car go. While I was in the car, I looked up and looked dead at the tractor parked on the side of our house. Remember, by this time, my daddy had the Alice Chandler tractor as well as his mule. He had warmed me many a time, saying, "Boy, don't you ever fool with this tractor; this thing will kill you." Needless to say, while everybody was talking, I slid away from the crowd and made my way to the tractor. When I got to the tractor, I said, "Boy, this is something; this is a real car here! Now if I can just get up there and get it cranked up!" Somehow, I managed to get up into the seat, and I remembered the stuff I had seen my daddy do; how he would turn the switch on, pull the little gas lever to give it gas. I did all that; I turned the switch on, and I saw the starter down on the floor, but my short leg could not reach it. Man! I reached down there; I tried to push, I could not push. I had to get to the end of the tractor seat as I tried my best to crank the tractor up. Finally, I held on to the steering wheel, and by holding on to the steering wheel, I was able to push down on the starter. The tractor started up; it went click, click, click, click, click, and somehow, everybody knew who it was that had backed out. The tractor started moving, but I did not know what to do. I was just looking at the tractor and holding onto the steering wheel. I saw my daddy coming. Everybody was hollering. I was scared, and the tractor was going toward the fence. My daddy jumped the fence, jumped on the tractor, which was going at a really slow pace, but fast enough to scare me. He stopped the tractor, pulled me off, and took off his belt. One can imagine what happened next. Here it was, his only day to rest, the only time he could have himself a good time, and I was getting into trouble again, trying to drive his tractor. He took that belt and wore me out; he put me on ice! I mean, he whipped the devil out of me! My Uncle Jesse felt sorry for me and said to my daddy, "Roland, don't hurt that boy! You know he just gets into a lot of things!" My daddy said, "Yeah! You can talk that stuff; you come here and spend a day or so and that's it, but this rascal wears us out! All day long, he's into something; I believe even when he is sleep, he may be into something. I have to wake up in the night to check that rascal out!"

Believe it or not, my daddy got some gravel from the road, took the gravel inside the house, spread the gravel on the floor, and made me get down on my knees on top of that gravel and stay there to pray until all of the company left. He came in from time to time to make sure I was on my knees. That was some kind of punishment, the worst kind of punishment, and when our company left, it was not over. My daddy wailed me out; I mean wailed me out! He made me haul in the wood, the chips for the wood and the water. He made me iron my pants and get my clothes ready to go to school the next day. He had really had it with me.

While I was growing up, I always had dreams of driving. I always wanted to drive, and I always wanted to go places. Maybe that's why I always got into mischief around the house. I was not a child to keep still like other kids who seemed content at home. I was never content at home. In fact, I never liked my surroundings. So, when I got the chance, I would go. That's why it stood to reason that I listened to Bubba's silly idea.

Bubba and I lived near each other; he lived on one side of the bayou, and I lived on the other side. Also, Bubba and I were in the same grade in school. Well, Bubba and I went to school one day, and I went with every intention of going to class as usual, but it just so happened that we had play time before school started for the day, and Bubba asked me if I had done my homework. I had not, and neither had he. So, I said, "We are going to get a beating this morning." I said that because in Catholic school, teachers would whip students if they did not have their homework. However, Bubba had a solution to our problem. He said, "Clabon, my cousin lives right here in New Roads; we can just walk around to their house." I hesitated and said, "I don't know about that!" He said, "Look, I tell you what, we'll be back at school before the bus leaves to catch the bus home." We lived six miles from the school, outside the town on False River, and the school was inside the city of New Roads. Thus, the bus was our means of getting to and from school.

Bubba's plan was that we would stay at his cousin's house all day, and just before school dismissed, we were going to go back to school and catch the bus home. I was very scared, but I let him talk me into it. We went to his cousin's house, and his cousin fed us real well. We played ball in the backyard and had a good time. We played and played and got carried away. When we realized it, it was four o'clock in the afternoon, and we knew we had missed the bus home. Of course, we had no choice but to walk the six miles home. By the time we got close to home, it had gotten dark, but I could see two figures walking towards me—figures that looked like my mama and daddy. As we walked on, it became clear to me that they were exactly who I thought they were—my mom and dad. My mama had a switch in her hand, and my daddy had what looked like a stick in his. When I saw that, my first thought was to duck down the lane to run, but I realized that it was getting late and dark. In reality, I had nowhere to go; Bubba quickly said, "You can't come to my house!" I did not know what to do. My daddy shouted, "You might as well bring your black 'so and so' here, because your behind belongs to me!" He said, "You might as well come on in here now; it's getting late." I replied, "Yeah, but y'all gonna whip me!" My daddy asked, "What are we going to whip you for?" I answered, "I don't know!" He yelled, "Well, where have you been all day?" I said, "It wasn't my fault; Bubba told me to come play hooky with him today; so we went over to his cousin's house." Man! When I said that, I saw stars! The expression is stars and stripes, but man! I saw stars, stripes, wipes, swipes, and sticks as they beat me. I mean, they whipped the living devil out of me; they whipped me into the house. All the other kids were looking at me; they had already eaten their dinner, and I guess I was their entertainment for the evening.

After my parents finishing beating me, I went up under the bed; as usual I was looking for shelter. My mama came to the bed and yelled, "Come out from under that bed; you've got to eat!" I came out from under the bed and was eating my food by the fireplace when my mama shouted, "Take that iron and start ironing your clothes for school" I started ironing my clothes, but I was watching for my dad because I knew that sometimes he would rebound on me and start whipping me again. While I was ironing my clothes, I was thinking that it was getting close to 9 o'clock; I knew that the later it got, the better it would be because everybody had to go to bed in order to be ready to go to work the next day. When I finished ironing my clothes, it was indeed time to go to sleep. My mama exclaimed, "You are not going to get in the bed to go to sleep; you are going to sleep underneath the bed!" I looked at her questioningly and said, "Underneath the bed?" During that time, I was still a kid and still scared of spooky situations; I was afraid, thinking about the stuff I had heard about ghosts. I knew that I would be scared to death underneath the bed. So I said, "No, Ma Moun, I don't want to sleep under the bed!" My daddy heard me and yelled, "Shut up, boy! Didn't you hear what your mama said?" I quietly answered, "Yes, sir. I'm sleeping under the bed right now." I grabbed a sheet and went under the bed. The next thing I knew, it was morning, and I had to get ready for school.

My mama, dressed in her apron and with a scarf tied around her head and ears to keep the air out, took me to school. She had gotten Reverend Bowie to drive us, and she had brought along her belt. She whipped me there at school, in my classroom right in front of all my classmates. I was greatly embarrassed by that, and I got a lot of teasing about it, too.

Bubba, my partner in crime, did not show up at school for two or three days after we had played hooky. When I did see him, I exclaimed, "Man, you got me in a world of trouble!" He replied, "Well, not me; I went and picked pecans for two days." It seems as if it had been okay for Bubba to ditch school, but it was not okay for me, that was for sure!

That afternoon when my daddy came home from the fields, I yelled, "See, daddy, I'm home!" He replied, "You better be home; as a matter of fact, as I think about it, I'm feeling pretty good today. I'm going to whip your butt again!" I said, "Oh, no; I'm not going to do it anymore!" He asked, "Are you sure you are not going to leave those school grounds anymore?" I said, "Yes, sir, I'm sure; don't hit me anymore; I'm going to keep still!" He half smiled and said, "Well, alright; go inside and do your chores."

It was not long after our day of playing hooky that Bubba quit school completely, and it seemed to have been no big deal with his parents. It was probably alright with them for him to quit because that meant that they would have one more field hand to help out and a little more money coming into their household.

By this time, I had reached the age of ten or eleven and was maturing somewhat and not getting into quite as much mischief as I previously had. My parents had started having me do more chores, and kept me from hanging around with Bubba since he was not in school. It was also around the time that we started being bothered with people poisoning our dogs and prowling around our house at night.

My father worked hard every day, and he was dead tired when he went to bed. He was also a sound sleeper, so he never heard the noises at night that frightened my mother, and she would not wake him from his rest. Frequently, my mother would hear somebody opening the front gate and walking on the gravel on the side of our house. What we later discovered was that somebody was sneaking around our house at night stealing food from the garden and the chicks and eggs from the backyard. One night, someone hit my parent's window with a rock or something. Well, I got mad and decided that I finally had enough of my mother being scared every night. I decided that I would shed a little light on the matter.

I took it upon myself to get some electrical wire, climb on top of the main power line pole, and connect the electrical wire to the main power line and run the wire from the pole, through the trees, all the way to the front corner of our house. I then took some nails and nailed the wires to the corner of the house. What I did was rig up an outdoor light that shined in the front of the house and on the side, all the way to the back on the side where my mama heard noises. I even went as far as to put a pan over the bulb to serve as a globe for the light so that the bulb would be protected when it rained.

When my father saw what I had done, he must have been satisfied with it because he did not whip me, and he did not say anything. We became accustomed to that light. In fact, that light stayed up for many years even after I had left home.

By now, it was the late 1950's; I was growing up, going through puberty, and getting more serious and mature about things. I had always been an inquisitive and observant child, and that did not change during this time. As a matter of fact, I would often listen to my parents talking, and I knew what hard times they were going through financially—how short their money was when the crops were bad. So I started wanting to help the family out. I started saving my money so that I could give them money because they were concerned about borrowing money and being in debt. I saved the money that I earned from working various odd jobs. I got jobs mowing and grooming people's lawns and working inside their homes. I did not like working inside their homes; I preferred working outside. Being inside got next to me because I would see all of their fancy clothes and stuff, and it would remind me too much of how poor we were and how they had gotten their stuff from basically being rogues, taking most of the money from us for themselves when we were the ones who did all the work.

I ended up asking Mr. Bourdeaux if I could work in his store, and he agreed that I could. So, I worked in his store putting canned goods on the shelves, putting coke bottles in their cases and doing different things. Working in the store was a good deal, especially in the winter when it was cold and rainy. I worked in the store during the off season, but I still had to chop and pick cotton and pull corn during harvesting time.

When I turned thirteen years old, I got a job with Pete's Pest Control. I met the owner, and he hired me to work around the pillars, digging the trenches at the houses that were being sprayed for termites and other pests. I worked at Pete's Pest Control for a little while and got bored.

It was getting close to Christmas, and I was not making that much money, so one Saturday, I walked the six miles to New Roads to see a man named Bubby Orlander who was the owner of a furniture store there in town. I felt confident that I could get a job at his store. I figured that I could either crush and stack the cardboard boxes after the furniture was taken out of them, or sweep the floor or do something. I was really gutsy about getting my hands on some money for Christmas. Luckily, Mr. Orlander hired me and I felt like a big guy because I was making $7.00 a day. Seven dollars a day was a lot of money for a kid to earn on a job back in those days. Another plus about working at the furniture store was that I had the privilege of going into town, and being in town was a big thing for me. It was a way of being away from the country, being away from my home and my surroundings. I felt good about that and about doing something positive on my own for myself.

After a while, my job played out at the furniture store, and everybody was in the middle of ballback times. Ballback times was a period when there was nothing to do. People would be loping around the countryside every day with absolutely nothing to do. During ballback times, I would wake up each morning, see dew on the ground, kids outside in the yard, cars passing by over on the road, and older men idling around. This dead period got my nerves so bad until I created something to do. I went across the way and got my friends Johnny and Tooter and told them that what we needed to do was go look for frogs. We scouted around and ended up killing about twenty-five or thirty frogs. The kind of frogs we killed were called spring chickens—big frogs that people used for fried frog legs, which was an expensive delicacy. We sold those frogs and made money.

I was always using my head to come up with ways to make money; killing and selling frogs was just one of the ways I came up with. Some of the white kids did the same thing, but for them, it was a way of playing and having fun; for me, it was serious business. I was trying to survive and better my condition. I even went down to The Lighthouse and asked Tooter's parents if I could launch the boats. I knew that if I helped people put their boats on the water, I would make myself some money. At every turn, I would look for ways to make money, and I continued throughout my adolescent years.

By now, it was 1967, and I was a junior in high school. The Vietnam War was escalating, and time was getting short for me to be at home. Of course, by this time I had started to look at young ladies. The prom was coming up, and I had to concentrate on saving my money to prepare myself to go to the prom. My big thing back then was to have a girlfriend. I only had one girlfriend in high school. Well, maybe I had two; or better yet, make that one and a half. There was one young lady that was my true girlfriend, and there was one who was sort of my girlfriend.

One of our favorite things to do as we dated back then was go to the fair. At the fair, I would meet my girlfriend and have a good time. The fair would come in the fall. After the fair would come Halloween, Thanksgiving, and then Christmas. I would prepare for all of those times, and before I realized it, the school year was over and I was entering the twelfth grade.

During my senior year, I continued to work. I worked in the fields. I also worked in the stores, and I continued to tell the different white guys who worked in town that I wanted to work with them again at Pete's Pest Control in Baton Rouge.

As things turned out, I had plenty of work, and when it was time to get ready for graduation, I paid for my graduation expenses. I bought my own graduation ring and cap and gown. I had earned enough money to pay for all of my graduation supplies.

Throughout my senior year, I found myself steadily listening to the news. I soon learned that the Vietnam situation was hot, really hot! It dawned on my mind that I would probably end up in that war. A few months before graduation, I got really anxious about things; I started wondering what I was going to do. I had decided that I wanted to be a builder, but I worried that I would not get a chance to carry out my plans. The rumor was that there was a list posted downtown, and if a guy's name appeared on the list, it was a sure thing that he would be drafted for the war.

Naturally, I went downtown to check out the list, and sure enough, my name was on the board. I was shocked when I saw it. When I saw my name printed there in black and white, I was actually startled. I immediately went home and told my parents that my name was up to be drafted, and they were surprised, also. They checked into it themselves when they went into town, but there was nothing they could do.

I was worried and upset. I even told my principal. I said to him, "Look, I'm just seventeen years old!" He said that there was nothing the he could do about my situation. So, it looked as if my fate was fairly set.

However, there were recruiters who came to our school and told us that if a person's name was on the draft list downtown, it would be better if that person went ahead and volunteered. They said that by volunteering, a guy would have an easier job and would not have to fight. Therefore, I volunteered, but what they told us was a lie—a big lie— because once a person's name was on the dotted line, Uncle Sam did whatever he wanted to do. Consequently, three days after I graduated from high school, they called me in for the entrance test. I deliberately tried to fail the test. In fact, I know I failed. There is no way possible that I passed, but they claimed that I passed it, and they quickly sent me to

New Orleans for a physical. After my physical in New Orleans, I was shipped straight to Fort Polk for basic training.

With all that had happened to me through the years, it seemed as if my life had gone from one extreme to another. The ground I had covered from my early childhood up until this time had been really rough, but little did I know of what lay ahead of me. I had no idea that the federal government already had my future planned out. My life had changed as quickly as one blinks an eye. I jumped from childhood into manhood really quickly, I mean like zap, and that was it! I was headed for Vietnam!

DESTINATION VIETNAM

BASIC TRAINING

My trip to Vietnam was by way of Fort Polk, Louisiana for basic training, as I mentioned earlier. In fact, it was just a few days after graduation that I was on a bus loaded with young guys headed for the same destination. The trip from home to Fort Polk was one long, uncomfortable journey. None of us got any sleep that night on the bus as we traveled to boot camp, and the next morning, the military personnel had us up bright and early. They had finished processing all of us by eight o'clock, and by nine o'clock, we were in formation where they had us lined up to start the preliminaries. They gave all of us the regular military treatment. They cut off all our hair, had us all shower, and also assigned us to our beds. The complete process was cut and dry, with no kindness or friendliness from anyone. As a matter of fact, the cold, callous procedures that I went through that first day seemed like pure hell to me. I had a real problem with the drill sergeant barking out orders about how we were to make our beds and keep our shoes shined and do everything. I had a little attitude within myself and wondered why he had to yell and holler out his instructions instead of talking to us in a normal tone of voice.

At the end of my first day at basic training, I, along with my fellow comrades, knew exactly what was expected of us and how we were to conduct ourselves. We knew how they wanted the beds made, how to stand at attention, how to stand at a parade rest, how to keep quiet, not mumble, scratch, or make any movement during formations. In that one day, they taught us a lot of stuff—basic military protocol regarding disciplined behavior—looking straight ahead, holding our heads straight and high, not looking to the left nor to the right, the usual military conduct. Even though they taught us all of this stuff, I am sure they knew that we were going to disobey orders, because we were street guys who had just come into the military and had to be taught all those military do's and don'ts.

Their teaching was the critical part for me because I was not too keen on taking orders and being commanded to do this and do that. Being bossed around went against my nature. So, to me, that first day's glimpse of basic training was just like getting a glimpse of hell.

If I thought the first day was bad, I got a real awakening the second day, which was the "pure de" training day. They woke us up at four AM for reveille; the drill sergeant came into our barracks and expected our beds to be made. Some guys did not have their beds made, so all of us had to get down and do pushups. On top of that, there were some guys in there who were very slow—guys that they obviously missed when they were giving us our physicals. Believe it or not, there were guys in basic training still wetting the bed. The sergeant would make those guys fall out of formation, drag their mattresses out and lay them out so that everybody could see them. Naturally, I looked and laughed at them, and sergeant yelled, "What'ya laughing at, soldier? Get down! Drop down there and give me fifty!" Once, I looked at the sergeant as if to say, "Give you fifty what?" When I looked around, I actually did ask, "Fifty what?" The sergeant answered with a bark, "Fifty pushups!" I dropped down and mocking yelled, "Fifty pushups; get down!" He immediately put his foot in my back, and I could barely do five pushups.

After the barrack inspection, they took us out running. We ran about a mile. They ran us hard to see who could stand up to the rigor. They wanted to know who would pass out, have a heart attack, an epileptic seizure, or some other ailment. If there were anything wrong with a person's body, they aimed to find out about it by having us run. We had to run without breakfast, right after we got up, made our beds, and donned our shined shoes.

The first time they ran us, they took us onto Southfolk, there on the base. A lot of the guys started vomiting, having headaches, passing out, and having all kinds of problems. Some of them had to return to Bravo 222, which was the unit I was in—Unit 222 B Company. Some guys just did not have the stamina and endurance to hold up under such demanding physical activity.

Each morning they ran us farther and farther. In a week's time, they had built us up to running four to five miles. During that week, we were either built up or weeded out. Those who were sick and weak with problems such as asthma or emphysema were identified and ultimately rejected. Those of us who were strong but just sore and tired were kept and built up through additional drills and training.

During drills and training, they had us doing a lot of low crawling, standing at attention, rope climbing, pole fighting, and all sorts of obstacle course running. The objective was to score 500 points to prove physical fitness. A score of 500 was the highest and the best. A score of 400-450 was good; a score of 375 was equivalent to a school grade of a C, and anything less than a 375 was considered failing, requiring that a person start over and repeat all of the drill and training routines. In other words, anyone making below 375 had to start basic training all over again. The drill sergeant let us know from the beginning what the expectations were so that we would have the incentive to do well.

Everybody's cry was, "Man, I've gotta get 500 points!" That was how the military brainwashed people.

As for me, I was shooting for my 500 points, but with all of the hollering and screaming from the drill sergeant, and him making me do pushups or putting me on K P for the least little thing I did, I had problems. I was the type of person who just flat out told the drill sergeants that I was not going to do certain things. One incident in particular that I remember occurred after a sergeant had drilled us and drilled us so hard and so fast in the grueling, hot sun, and I simply told him that I was not going to do it anymore. His name was Sergeant Stokes from Clinton, Louisiana, a little town about five miles from my hometown (although I did not know that at the time). When I refused to drill any longer, Sergeant Stokes told me to drop down and give him fifty. I looked him straight in the eyes and held my ground. When I looked at him so defiantly, he said, "Soldier, didn't I tell you to get down? When I tell you to get down, get down!" He grabbed me, put my hands behind my back, slapped me, pushed me down, and yelled, "Give me fifty!" I started to jump on him then, that very day, but I did not. He had his foot in my back, and I was doing the pushups, but I was getting really mad and the tension and anger were building up inside me. He kept looking at me as I did the pushups, and he could see the sternness and anger in my eyes.

When these military men, the drill sergeants, knew that a person was one of those hard cats who would not do what he was told to do, they dealt with that person even more harshly. They would take their good time and cut the person up and try and break his spirit, and that is exactly what they did to me after the pushup incident.

That same night, when I had fire duty and had to be on guard for an hour, Sergeant Stokes watched me like a hawk the whole time that I was on duty. He kept his eyes on my every move, and when I finished my duty and left, he left.

It was the very next day that Sergeant Stokes called me out of formation and told me to drop down and do fifty. I told him that I wasn't going to do anything. He immediately asked, "What did you say, soldier?" I said, "I'm not going to do a damn thing. By the way, this is what I'm going to do!" And I jumped on him like somebody crazy, knowing that I could not beat this man, with him knowing and using all kinds of karate and fighting techniques. Yet, I gave him a pretty good whipping, but even so, I still could not beat him. By the time I had finished scuffling with Sergeant Stokes, another drill sergeant came up and kicked me to the side and fractured my leg. That is how I ended up with a fractured leg during basic training.

But even with that fractured leg, I still had to train and do the exercises. I did not have to run, but I had to do everything else. As it was, I was a country boy, so running had never been a big deal for me; I could always run. The more they made us run, the more I ran with no problems.

Even with my fractured leg, I ended up with over 400 points that week and got to go home on a weekend pass, which surprised me because guys who were disobedient and broke the rules were often denied weekend passes. Yet, I was able to go home on a weekend pass, and, of course, I told my parents that the drill sergeant broke my leg. Knowing me, I am sure I did not give them all the specifics of what led up to the sergeant breaking my leg.

Sure, I was hardheaded and rebellious, but I was not alone. There were a lot of guys who were rebellious and would not follow orders and who ended up being kicked out of service because the military could not do anything with them. Also, there were a lot of guys who were really tough and actually kicked some drill sergeants' behinds. There were a lot of physically strong and headstrong guys in service. Some of them got dishonorable discharges; some got general discharges.

Although I was one of the headstrong, rebellious guys, for some reason they worked with me until they broke me in. when they broke me in, I really started taking my training seriously and started running and doing what I was supposed to do. Sergeant Stokes saw this change in me, and another drill sergeant who worked with us saw it, too. They also saw that I was a good runner. Subsequently, they used me as a leader of the pack, which I did not want to be because that meant that I had to always be up front, singing cadence, such as, "See the woman in black; she makes her living on her back!" And the guys in the back of me had to sing a reply, "See the woman in red; she makes her living in bed!" That was our cadence, and I did not like having to lead it. Nevertheless, that is what I had to do, and basic training continued to be an okay experience for me. We kept running, and I proved to be in top-notch physical condition.

Sergeant Stokes had made me a leader, but I was still angry with him because he had not let up on me; he was still making me do countless pushups and constantly coming down on me about everything. I could not understand why he was still bearing down on me; I was doing my exercises and pushups and everything that I was supposed to be doing, but he was still pressing me, and I was furious!

One day, I got so mad until my head was just steaming and it felt like it was turning into a red vessel about to blow up. I knew I could not fight Sergeant Stokes because I wanted to go home on a weekend pass, and I knew I would lose that privilege if I jumped him, since taking away a weekend pass was one of the main methods the drill sergeants used to make us soldiers obey them and do as we were told.

Even though I knew all this, I had reached my boiling point that day, and I said, "See, you! I'm going to kill you!" I told Sergeant Stokes that and went on to say, "Wait until we get to the firing range." He asked, "What did you say, soldier?" I said, "I'm going to kill your ass when we get to the firing range! I'm going to get you one way or the other. You are the reason for my fractured leg, and I'm going to get you for this. You are just drilling me and drilling me!" He replied, "Oh, you are going to do that?" Whop! He hit me hard and made me get down and do 200 pushups. On top of that, he made me get into what is called a dying cockroach position, and believe me, that is a position that no one would want to be in. it was lying down on my side on my elbow, stretched still without bending. He forced me to keep that position until I cried. My body was in deep stress, and I was hurting and in great pain. I mean, he really drilled me!

By this time, basic training was in full force. We had gotten to the point where we had to go to the firing range, but before doing that, we had to learn how to break our weapons down, clean them, and put them together again with precision and speed. I liked doing that because I am mechanically inclined, and I was good at it. I could break my weapon down and put it back together in no time-in ten or fifteen seconds fat. Sergeant Stokes would watch me out of the corner of his eye. He would watch me and a few other guys, white and black guys. I liked that; I liked knowing that he was impressed with my skills. He kept on watching me because he could see how well I was doing, but he would never give me credit for it. That made me mad all over again. We were told that our goal was to become expert marksmen with our weapon. My thought was that I wanted to be an expert with all of the weapons, and I did accomplish that.

When we finally got to the firing range, I noticed that Sergeant Stokes was not there. He had been taken out of the line-up for training us. I immediately remembered that I had threatened to kill him. I had made the threat when I was really mad, and apparently they did not want to take any chances on what might happen. Much to my surprise, a white drill sergeant was in charge at the range.

I succeeded in becoming an expert; I was an expert with the M-14. Three white guys, two other black guys, and I were the top guys. I came out as expert with the 45, M-14, and M-16. I could not zero the M-16, but I zeroed the M-60 and the M-50 as an expert and got all the medals that are on my jacket still to this very day.

Near the end of training, after spending a considerable amount of time on the firing range, I went back to the hootch. I saw Sergeant Stokes, and I just looked at him when I passed by him in the mess hall, the lunchroom. He just looked at me, but the point was that whenever we went to the firing range, they would not let him and me mix together. Yet, when it came to the training, he was down on me! Every morning when we ran, he would holler, "Jones!" Somebody would say, "What Jones?" since there were a lot of guys by the name of Jones. Sergeant Stokes would yell, "Jones, Clabon Jones!" "Darned it, man!" I would mumble under my breath. He would call me up front, and invariably someone would say, "He's dealing you, man!" I would go up and lead the pack as we ran anywhere from ten, twelve, or thirteen miles. We ran from Southfolk to Northfolk, singing and running.

After rigorous running, we would go in for exercises and more training—low crawling, doing the bars—all kinds of exercises. Training also included being thrown in the gas chamber. They wanted to see if we could function under the influence of the gas; the test was to see if we could say our social security number. Needless to say, going through the gas chamber was a horrible ordeal, I guarantee that! Snot would come out of my nose, my eyes would water, and the drill sergeants would come in and out, trying to make me talk. I had to say my social security number because they would not let up until I could say my name and social security number.

About a week before the end of basic training, I was doing fine; my leg was better, I was doing my exercises, and I was making my 500 points. Nevertheless, during the final week, the week prior to graduation, Sergeant Stokes was still drilling me unmercifully. He drilled me until that Thursday. At this point in the game, I had resolved within my mind to be cool. The exact words that I thought to myself were, "I'm going to leave this Negro alone. I'm going to leave this Negro alone and get him off my mind because it's just days before my graduation!"

On this Thursday, before all this stuff would be over, I had finished all of my work and training and was on the back porch of my little dorm, resting, I was looking at my girlfriend's picture and trying to write her a letter when Sergeant Stokes came up and scared me. He came up quietly from behind, and he actually frightened me. Of course, when an officer came up, I knew to stand at attention. So, I immediately jumped to attention. He said, "At ease, soldier." I replied with a polite, "Yes, sir!" But I was mad at him. Then, he asked me what I was doing, and I answered that I was writing my girlfriend and getting ready to write my mama. In my mind I was saying, "What the hell do you want?" He continued the conversation by casually saying, "You're Jones, Clabon Jones." I said, "You know me." He went on to comment that I was from a town called New Roads, Louisiana. I corrected him and said that I was not exactly from New Roads, that New Roads was the nearest town to Oscar, Louisiana, which was where I was really from. He then asked if it would make me feel any better to know that he was from Clinton, Louisiana. I will admit that that did peak my interest, but I nonchalantly said, "Oh, you are from Clinton, Louisiana?" He then asked if I had any people going to Southern University. I told him that I had brothers and sisters going to Southern. He commented that Southern was right down the street. I curtly said, "Yea, I know where Clinton is." Then, he said something that shocked me. He said, "By the way, you're a mighty good soldier." I said, "Well, you sure didn't act like it by the way you treated me." He replied, "Well, let me just tell it to you now, now that you are graduating, and it's just you and I here and we're homeboys." I said, "Homeboys?" in a questioning tone. He said that, yes, we were homeboys because I was from New Roads, and he was from Clinton. He said that he had dated a young lady from New Roads and thought that there were real good people in New

Roads. In fact, his statement was that he liked those Creole people from New Roads.

At this point, we had gotten deep into a good conversation, and I went on to tell him that we had lots of fun in New Roads, that it was a nice countryside, that the river was nice, and if people got tired of the field, they could go to the river. Then, he explained something to me. He said, "The reason I was training you so hard like I was, private, is that when I found out that you were from my home area, I had to make sure that you were well built. You were already built by your physical structure, but I had to make sure that your body was really built." He said this jokingly, and I laughed and asked, "What do you mean?" He then replied, "Have you heard the Chevrolet commercial?" I answered, "No." He said, "Well, I just had to make sure your body was 'officially built' to stand up under the pressure, just like they talk about in the Chevy commercial. In other words, I had to make sure that you were in good shape before you go over to Vietnam because I've been there. Now, look at your body; just look at how you are built!" I said, "I was already built." He replied, "No, now you've got muscles; your neck is straight and everything is in shape." He went on to say that the reason he had been so rough on me was that he did not want to see me go to Vietnam and be like some of the guys who were out of shape who could not run and would sometimes give up and give out. Sergeant Stokes explained that he saw that I had what he called a "little nick" in me and I was quick. He said, "I had to teach you how to control your temper, and I had to train you because I want you to be a good soldier to be able to come back home to your folks." He continued by reminding me that I would be going to infantry training next. He said that if I thought his training was hard, I should wait until I got to infantry school, and I would see that the training there was going to be very intense. He said that when I got to Northfolk he was going to come and check me out. Then, in all seriousness, he decided to give me some heartfelt advice. He said, "Let me tell you something. Vietnam is the place you are headed to; You are going to see some tragic things, and your body must be prepared; you must be prepared. You don't have time to joke around while we are trying to train you. This is why I drilled you and I drilled you, and I got all of the crud out of your mind so that you could focus on cleaning that gun, cleaning that gun, and putting that gun back together again as fast as you can because your life will depend upon it—everything you do here, your life will depend upon in Vietnam. That's why I was so hard on you!" He went on to say that the threat I made on his life could have gotten me put away if he had reported it, but chose not to because he knew it was just a lot of talk—"baby talk" is how he described it. He said that he knew that I was just angry at that time. He then asked, "You wouldn't have really shot me, would you?" Naturally, I said, "No." I explained that I was mad, just like he said. He said he realized that it was hot out in the training field, and things were rough. He told me not to be anybody's fool and to get as much training as I could in my classes, to listen in my classes and do all the exercises, and even when I did not have to exercise, to go out and exercise anyway.

Sergeant Stokes and I talked like that for some time that Thursday evening. When he was about ready to leave, he said, "You know, besides all of this Army stuff, Jones, I really like you; you're a unique guy. I noticed you when your leg was broken, how you kept on doing your hurdles, your running, rope climbing and all your training. You have good qualities in you. Use them to your advantage. I'm not going to talk to you any more until graduation. I'll see you on the firing range!" I quickly asked, "On the firing range, are you going to be out there?" He smiled and said, "Yeah, I'm going to be out there, and now you will have a chance to kill me if you want to." I sheepishly replied, "Oh, no, I said that at that particular time, but I wouldn't really do that to you." That's when he grabbed me around my shoulders and said, "I know that! I'll be checking on you when you get to Northfolk."

So, that was that, and I graduated from basic training a few days later. The military gave me a fourteen day leave back before I left infantry training. I really needed and appreciated that leave time because I had already been warned about infantry school.

INFANTRY SCHOOL

Lord have mercy! Indeed! I soon discovered that infantry training was totally different from basic training. Even the way they had the camp set up for us was completely different. Basic training was like drinking milk; infantry training was like drinking "pure de" straight alcohol; I am serious! They immediately had us go on what was called Biffwack. The training was something else! As soon as we got there, the people jumped on us, hollering and screaming. They had us doing about ninety things. They screamed, "Put down your sacks; give me fifty pushups; give me a hundred, two hundred pushups!" It seems to me that in that one day, they had us do a thousand things; they had us rocking and rolling.

There was no doubt about it; infantry training was really rough. Winter was setting in, also, which did not help matters. Some of the training was the same type that we had gotten at boot camp, but it was rougher and harder. They expected us to have learned the little nicks and basic stuff at boot camp, so they just drilled us and drilled us. They made us run and run and run. If I had to measure it in actual distance, I believe it would have amounted to me running from the Atlantic to the Pacific. No kidding, I truly believe that it would have been that much distance, because I ran thousands of miles. The intent was to drill us and drill us to teach us how to survive.

One evening, they threw us out into the field in the blistering cold. I was freezing! They gave us a raw chicken and some C4. We had to find a way to cook that chicken if we wanted to eat that night. They gave us bags to sleep in, and it was bitter cold. Late into the night, they woke us up and gave us maps that we had to use to find our way back to our perimeter. The maps were not that well defined, colorful maps that we see in stores; these maps were maps of the jungle. We had to learn how to use those maps and how to grid coordinates.

In the midst of teaching us all about maps, they taught us many other survival skills. They taught us unity, how to be together, how to stick together and how to respect each other. They taught us all about the different types of terrain and how to cope in any environment. Moreover, they taught us how to make bombs, how to hook up Claymore Mines, how to kill others and how to do away with ourselves if we had to in a situation where we thought we would not make it. They stressed that if things came to that, then it would be a decision that we would have to make on our own. They taught us how to help our fellow man if he got shot—how to carry him. They taught us how to use our pistols effectively or our 45's if we did not have our M-16, M14, M-60 or our 79 grenade launchers with us. Even beyond all of that, they taught us how to fight with our hands if we had no weapon. We had to fight each other; I mean actually fight each other with sticks and with our bare hands. We were trained how to rescue in choppers, how to tote a wounded man. We were also trained on what to do if one of our men were killed; we were taught to open his mouth and throw the dead soldier's dog chain in his mouth, or if we had time, we were instructed to tie the dog chain to his big toe. Virtually, what it all boiled down to is that at infantry school, they taught us how to survive when we got to Vietnam, and how to die if necessary.

We not only had outside training, but also had inside classes where they lectured us, and we got more lessons about the Vietnam climate and terrain. The main emphasis was on teaching us grid coordinates. That was very, very important; we had to learn grid coordinates! They would give us maps that had nothing but green on them. We had to get our maps and figure out the clicks we needed if we had to throw bombs at a certain area. There was no getting around learning this essential skill.

In infantry school we had all kinds of classes—obedience classes, classes to teach us how to eat standing up straight, classes to teach us how to walk when we walked around the compound. We could not walk slumped over like we did not care, we had to walk with our heads up, straight and tall. In addition to all of this, there were also other restrictions placed upon us. We had to be neat and clean; we could not throw any paper on the grounds. If a soldier threw as much as a cigarette butt on the ground, he had to pick it up, go dig a grave someplace, and bury that cigarette butt. The bottom line was that no one could throw paper on Uncle Sam's grounds. The military would make a person dig a six foot grave to bury a cigarette butt, and also make him say a prayer over the grave after the cigarette butt was buried. The procedure was just like somebody burying a human being. Yet, Uncle Sam would go a step further because they would make a soldier turn right around and dig the cigarette butt up. This might sound crazy and funny, but that is exactly what would happen. The soldier would have to dig until he found the buried butt. He would then have to take the cigarette butt out of the grave and cover that big hole back up. After he did all of this, he had to go find a trash can and put the cigarette butt in the trash can. Almost the same thing would happen if a soldier spit on the ground. No, nobody was supposed to spit on Uncle Sam's ground. Of course, I say Uncle Sam meaning the government, because Uncle Sam was by no means my uncle. But the point is that nobody was supposed to spit on the military's ground. If he did, he had to dig the spit up with hands, put the spit in a trash can, and then cover the hole up that was made when he dug up the spit. Plus, this spit digging was not the real punishment. The real punishment was having to exercise, of course, nothing but exercise—nothing but pushups, low crawls, back crawls, the bars, and having to get into the dying cockroach position.

By now, the picture should be clear about what took place at infantry school. We were taught everything—how to be clean, to have our shoes spit shined, and how to have our barracks spic and span. When a sergeant walked in, everything was to be in order. If it took us helping a buddy with his bed, or whatever, we did it because we knew that if one man had to go, then the whole crew had to go. We were all taught that no matter what a man was—black, white, Mexican, Honduran, Jamaican— we had to stick together because when we got to Vietnam, that was what we would have to do.

Luckily, I made it through infantry training, but the training was super intense. Some of the guys who made it through basic training just could not make it in infantry. Some got dishonorable discharge, some got general discharges, and some just skipped out. When they got their weekend passes, they never returned.

I graduated from infantry school with high points; I had my 500 points, and I became an expert with the M-60, M-16, 45, M-14 and M-79 Grenade Launcher. I also had zeroed in the Law.

I almost forgot about the Law. A funny thing happened when they were training us with the Law. I was standing at the back of the Law, and the drill sergeant asked me where I would stand to shoot the gun. I told him that I would stand behind it because I did not want to get shot. He said, "Son, come to the side; soldier, come to the side please and let me show you what will happen." When that guy pulled that trigger, my eyes got as big as Chicago, Illinois, because I saw that that thing had a big blast; it had a back blast that could kill just as well as the front blast could.

All in all, in infantry school we got a lot of training—top training. No matter how intense the training was and no matter what we said or what we called the drill sergeants, I realized that all that training was for us to get better to go Vietnam in order to conquer the jungles—those unknown jungles, places that we had never put our feet in before. The training taught me so much. It built up my mind; it taught me a lot of discipline and how to listen. Infantry training taught me how to have a quick mind, to be quick thinking, how to save my fellowman, how to have respect for the dead, how to have respect for the dying, and how to have respect for the living. I also learned how to have respect for the high officers over me. I realized that if they were over me, they evidently knew what they were doing. I equate it to the same thing that happens in a person's church home. If God picks a shepherd to preach in the church, people should shut up and listen. I found that people should listen because the message God gives the shepherd to preach on Sunday can be taken to live on for the whole week, just like the training I received from the sergeants was used to take me through Vietnam.

When I got out of training, I had discovered that in this world, it was all about parental training and guidance. When a person has that, he can go a long, long way. It all came down to discipline, too. Obeying, doing what is right, doing your best. I discovered that I should pay no attention to what the other man was doing, but do what I was told to do while under orders. Again, I think that it is the same way with the Bible. If we would just keep the Ten Commandments (I call that basic training), we would be prepared and be here to see the Rapture come, and we would be in the Rapture, as well.

After infantry school graduation, I had another fourteen day leave. I spent it partying. I went to a club called Bird Satellite Lounge, and I had a good time. I also spent time going back and forth from Baton Rouge to Oscar to visit my parents. I hung out in Baton Rouge because I had brothers and sisters at Southern University. I mostly used my fourteen days going out on Saturday nights, trying to enjoy myself.

VIETNAM BOUND

When my fourteen days were up, it was the beginning of what seemed like the end for me. It was a time of mixed emotions. I had numb feelings; I was scared about leaving home and leaving my family. My mind flashed back to all of my childhood experiences—how my daddy used to whip me, how I thought that I was bad, but how my daddy said that I was not bad, just mischievous. He assured me that I was not bad, just curious and aggressive, which caused me to get into a lot of jams.

On my last day at home, my mama cooked breakfast for me that morning while I put on my clothes, getting ready to leave. My dad did not go to work that morning because he wanted to see me off. He went outside and fed chickens and did various chores, but he kept looking at me and asking me if I were alright.

When I finished dressing, I ate my breakfast. Different people were coming by, and my brothers and sisters were all there. Everybody kept looking at me; everywhere I put my eyes, they were all looking at me. My daddy was really looking. My mama was, too. She was already sick with sugar diabetes, high blood pressure, gallstones, and a goiter that choked her in the throat. She did not want to see me go. My sisters and brothers were nonchalant, but they knew I was going into a bad situation.

During all this commotion on the morning of my departure, a strange thing happened. The TV was on and the news was on, and they were talking about Vietnam. They were announcing the casualties as they always did. At that moment, my mind started flicking back to the good times I had, to all the adventures I had in my childhood—my getting bit by a snake, getting pecked in the eye, driving the tractor, my mama pulling a gun on me, making me stay in the yard when I wanted to go and play with the rest of the kids. My mind recalled all the laughter, the fun, the fights I got into at school. It was like one big ball going around in my head as I reflected on my earlier life. I was sitting at the kitchen table thinking about all the times I had run in and out of house, watching this same TV, hearing about Vietnam. I sadly realized that now, it was my time to go.

After I finished my breakfast, it was time for me to leave. My brother was driving me to Baton Rouge to Ryan Airport. We were out in the yard; neighbors came by to shake my hand and say goodbye. I noticed that my daddy was still looking at me while he was standing on the porch. My brother snapped a picture of me, which I still have. I was hugging my mama and my sisters and saying goodbye. My eye went to the corner, and I saw my daddy, just looking straight at me. I broke away from the crowd and started toward him; he met me half way. He was not crying, but he grabbed me tightly and said, "Boy, don't you eat nothing over there that the United States Army doesn't feed you! Don't trust those people; eat only the food that Uncle Sam feeds you; do you hear me? You be good. From my understanding, you have been well trained. Use your head; don't fool with no drugs." I said, "Yes, sir!" to all of his well-intended advice.

Finally, I got in the car and we pulled away. I looked at my mother and father. They were looking at me as if to say, "Don't go!" As we were driving off, I realized that I would not see my parents for a whole year or more. My eyes and head got heavy. My eyes got real watery. My brother was steadily talking; I heard him, but I was not listening. My mind was in other places. We had a forty-five minute to an hour's ride to Ryan Airport.

When we got to Ryan, there was the jet, a Delta jetliner, already there. I took a picture of that jet, which I also still have. That jet was going to take me from Baton Rouge, and then on to Houston. I was going to take another, bigger jet (a 747) from Houston to Oakland, California.

I boarded the jet. I had never been on one before. I looked around and discovered that it was really nice inside. I did not know how I was going to feel riding the thing. Soon, they closed the door, the lights came on, and the jet started backing up and going down the strip. I started looking out of the window; for some reason, I always sat by a window. Shortly, the jet took off. I was not really scared. Actually, I do not know how to describe the feeling I had.

The next thing I knew we were in the sky, and we were so far up that I was completely amazed. I touched one guy and said, "That's a cloud down there, isn't it?" He replied, "It sure is; that's exactly what it is. Is this your first time flying?" I answered, "Yes." Then he asked me where I was headed, and I said that I was headed to Vietnam. He responded with, "Oh, gosh! Why did I have to ask you that?" He and I continued to have a little conversation, and before I knew it, we were landing in Houston.

I had not flown before so I did not know how to use a terminal. Of course, all I had to do was go to the Delta counter and find out about my connecting flight. The military told me that I had to change jets, but that was confusing to me, and I was not sure what to do. Luckily, one of the guys who worked at the airport showed me what line to get in and everything to do and it all worked out.

I had a little time in Houston. Actually, I ended up waiting there for about an hour. Then, I got on this big, humongous jet which turned out to be a Boeing. We immediately took off from Houston. We were told that we had a three and a half to four-hour hike to Oakland. It was a beautiful day. That jet got on top of the clouds, and we were just flying! I was busy looking at all the seats on the jet. One of the stewardesses came by and asked if I wanted anything to drink; I didn't. I was too busy observing and taking everything in. I noticed that they had radios on the sides of the seats. I was engrossed, looking around and out of the window; things looked beautiful from up there in the skies. A movie came on, but I was not very interested in looking at the movie that they were showing. I was just riding along as we chugged along.

I remember when we passed over the Grand Canyon, they pointed it out to us, and I was excited because I had heard so much about it. When I looked down, I saw the depth of the Canyon and the steep mountains surrounding it as the jet flew away, allowing us a better view. We kept flying, with me continuously looking out the window all the way until we got to Oakland.

Finally, we arrived in Oakland, and when we got there, what scared me was that I did not know how to swim. The jet landed on a strip right over the water. First, there was the water, and then the strip. I saw that and realized that we were flying mighty low to that water, and that scared me. When the jet hit the strip, I could not see it, and I thought we had hit the water.

When I deboarded the jet, the Army people themselves were there waiting for me. They put me on a Jeep and escorted me to Edwards Air Force Base in Oakland California. At the base, they assigned me to my room, where I discovered that there was not much to do. There was no sergeant there to drill me or holler at me as I had been accustomed to, and I must admit that that did put me a little at ease. They gave me my little room with my bed in it, and I peddled around the place, drinking orange juice and settling into the new environment.

There at Edwards Air Force Base, the only thing I had to dodge were pots and pans, because they were always trying to get someone to wash dishes. I learned that real quickly and got away from it.

After I got situated, one of the first things I did was call my cousins there in Oakland. I wanted to go see them, but somehow that did not work out. I did go to see my great uncle who was very sick. He told me that he was going to pray for me because he wanted me to make it back from Vietnam safely. After my visit with my uncle, I went back to the base, and the next day it was time for us to make preparations to depart from the United States.

The military had all of us getting our passports straightened out and getting all of papers in order. We had to sign papers saying who we wanted our money to go to in case we got killed. We had to complete forms if we wanted an allotment of our pay to be sent home. We had to fill out all kinds of forms—insurance, information forms about personal things such as whether we had wives and children and so forth. We went through that paperwork drill practically all day. Then, on the following day, we got ready for the actual departure to Vietnam.

They lined us up and called each of our names to be sure we all had our papers. They loaded us all up on a deuce and quarter (a truck) and took us farther out on the base. When we got to the designated spot, I was in awe of the jets that I saw there.

Those jets were the largest jets that I had ever seen in my life! They looked like big bulldogs to me because I had not seen jets so huge. They called them seawater horses because they only traveled overseas. Those jets were never seen in certain parts of the United States; they were basically only in the coastal areas. Those jets had big humps in the back of them; each jet had three engines on one side, three on the other side, and one big engine in the middle, on top of the fuel lodge. I mean that those were extraordinarily big jets!

Now, what got to me was that I was standing up there watching one of the jets when all of a sudden, the bottom started coming down real slowly to the ground. That's what I noticed that there was a big hole in the jet, somewhat like a ramp, where everything went inside of it. As I continued to look, I saw that there were tanks parked on the sidelines, and there were deuce and quarters lined up, also. I did not know what the trucks had in them, but the tanks and trucks were all lined up and waiting.

I kept watching, and the next thing I saw were the tanks crawling up and going inside the jet. Then, I saw the Jeeps go inside. I was puzzled and amazed. I scooted over to a lieutenant and said, "Yeah, man, this thing here is going to burst open with all of this stuff going up in it. Jeeps are going up there, and there are tanks on this thing!" He replied, "Oh, yeah, yeah. We're just loading up." I then asked, "Is this jet going to take off with all of this here on it?" His reply was, "Of course!" I could not believe it; Jeeps, trucks and tanks were on that jet. They had even driven what looked like a presidential car onto it, as well.

As we watched all of those vehicles being put onto the jet, there was murmuring among the soldiers. I, for one, was wondering in my mind if that was the jet we were going to be on, also, and if so, I could not imagine where we were going to fit among all those Jeeps and other stuff. I just did not know; I had no idea about what was going on there. Then, another deuce and quarter pulled up, and some of the soldiers who worked there on the base started unloading caskets from it on to the jet.

My gut reaction was, "Oh, no! Wait a minute!" I was upset to say the least. I went back to one of the captains and asked, "Why are they putting caskets on this thing? Is this the same jet we are going to go on?" He answered, "Yes!" Then, I exclaimed, "You mean to tell me these tanks, these Jeeps, and now these caskets, are being put on this time, and this is the jet we are going to go on?" He said, "Yelp!" I then asked, "Why are they carrying caskets over there?" He looked around, and he looked at me and said, "Well, soldier, the live bodies go, and the dead ones come back." I said, "You aren't talking about us, are you?" His answer was, "Well, if you aren't going to make it back alive, maybe one of them could be for you, or for someone aren't going to make it back alive, maybe one of the casket could be for them, or one could be for me." I yelled, "Wait a minute! These things here, we can't travel with caskets!" I had pretty much forgotten about the Jeeps and other things I had seen loaded on the jet. My focus was on those caskets. The captain said that the caskets were for the dead bodies that came back to the States. He went on to explain that every time a jet went over to Vietnam, there would be a shipment of caskets sent back. I was hysterical; I said, "I can't believe this!" They continued loading the caskets, and eventually the bottom of the jet was filled with tanks, Jeeps, the presidential looking car and the caskets. They then made us soldiers get into formation. Man, I mean it was a gang of us, about 250 or so. All of us had to board that jet. We were supposed to fit into the top section, much to my amazement.

As we were getting ready to load up, I was thinking, "I'm not going to get on this thing because this thing is not going to leave the ground. There is no way this thing can pick up all this weight! There are too many of us, not to mention the Jeeps, tanks, and other vehicles. That is too much already; then they have loaded the dog gone thing up with caskets, and now they want to load about 250 of us on there! Naw! Naw!! I cannot take that!"

While we were standing in line, a sergeant passed by, and I asked, "Sergeant, man, have y'all ever tried this before?" He said, "What'ya talking about, soldier?" I answered, "Have y'all ever tried taking all this in a jet before?" He looked at me and said, "Attention! Get on board, solider, go on up and get on board!" Well, I had no choice; I had to go ahead and get on board. I climbed the stairs—a lot of steps way to the top of the jet. When I got inside, it looked like a huge house inside. That's how large it was; it had six seats on one side and six seats on the other side and three seats in a row in the middle. I mean that thing was huge inside! I got a seat next to a sergeant. The air conditioning was running, and I was real scared, very scared. This sergeant and I did not talk at first; I was looking around and kind of kept to myself. I felt like I might have been making a fool of myself by asking so many questions, but I also thought that I couldn't be a fool because in my mind, that thing was not going to take off from the ground. As they closed all the doors and everything, I heard the engines gearing up. I kept looking outside and hearing the engines making all of this noise. Everything was real slow, and it looked as if each engine was bigger than a car. I have an LHS New Yorker, and it seemed like each engine was bigger than that car. Finally, the jet started moving, and it moved around onto the strip to take off. It looked to me as if we rode about ten miles to take off. I touched the sergeant seated beside me and asked, "Is this thing going to go up?" He started laughing and said, "Yes, it's going to go up." The jet kept chugging down the strip, and I could hear the engines simmering. I gripped my seat so tightly until, I imagine, that my fingerprints are still in that seat if that jet is in operation today. I had my seat gripped so tightly that, if we had crashed, that seat would have had to come out of the metal it was bolted into. The jet continued to move, and I could hear cracking sounds; then all of a sudden it took off, and it was like I was floating in the air. That rascal took off slowly; it did not take off fast like the others I had seen at Stateside. It went slowly, clean into the sky.

By this time, it had gotten dark, and we were on our way. As the jet leveled off, I spoke to the guy sitting next to me and discovered that our first stop would be Hawaii. I asked him if we really had to land the thing a second time; I wanted to know if we couldn't just wait until we got to Vietnam before we landed again. His reply was that we had to stop in Hawaii to refuel and have the jet checked out. I asked if we had to unload in Hawaii, and he said that we did not have to unload—everything we had on board, the baggage and all would stay on board. At that, I asked, "Then why do they have to check it?" He calmly answered that they had to check and refuel the jet. With that, I said, "Okay then!" and we traveled on.

When we got to Hawaii, we had gained time; it was still daylight. We landed, and the strangest thing was that it was a smooth landing. We pulled into the terminal area, and they let us deboard the jet. The Hawaiians were putting these flowered wreaths around the soldiers' necks, which was also strange to me. I wondered if they were going to put one around my neck. When I got up to them, I bent my head down, and a lady put one of the wreaths around my neck, too. I went inside the terminal where they were selling alcohol and all kinds of stuff. However, I did not drink at that time so I did not take too much notice of the bars. We stayed at the terminal for about two hours while they were checking the jet.

Finally, we reboarded and took off again. I had my same assigned seat. Most of the soldiers looked like they had settled in and were relaxed by this time, but the sergeant next to me must have noticed that I was still on the wondering side of things because he touched me and asked, "What are you doing on this jet? You look mighty young!" I replied that I was of age—eighteen years old and I had been drafted. He then asked if my parents knew that I was going to Vietnam. I said that of course they did. He asked if they had signed for me to go, and I told him that they had not because I was of age. I offered to show him my papers, but he told me that I did not have to do that. Yet, I showed them to him anyway. Then, I asked him who he was; he told me his name which I have forgotten, and he told me that this was his second time going to Vietnam. He proceeded to tell me a little about his childhood and the reason he stayed in 'Nam. He told me that he really didn't have a family or a home or anything like that. I told him that this was my first and last time going to Vietnam. In fact, I said, "I don't appreciate going now!" He smiled and asked me what my military occupation was. I told him infantry. He replied, "Oh, no!" That puzzled me, so I asked, "What's that?" He said, "Going over here, infantry can be one of the worst jobs you can have!" I asked him what his MO was, and he said that he was a military policeman. He went on to ask me if I really knew what I was going into. My answer was no, and I went on to tell him that I had never left home before. I had no idea that I would be fighting a war at this point in my life.

We continued talking, and he asked me where I was from. I told him that I was from Louisiana—the bauya country. He started laughing at me, and I asked him what was wrong. He said that he could tell that I was from down South, from the country. I asked how that was, and he said because I had said that I was from the "bauya" country. I wanted to know what was wrong with that, and he told me that most southern said "bauya" when it's really bayou.

This sergeant then asked me again if I were sure that my parents knew that I was headed to Vietnam. I hastily replied that they did and reminded him that I had shown him my papers. By this time, it was obvious that he was picking fun at me, and he continued by saying that I was a tough little man. I told him that I was trying to be one. Our conversation paused then as he started to look out of the window.

I interrupted the sergeant's concentration and asked, "Is this jetliner going to stay up in the sky with all this stuff we got on it?" He smirked, laughed and said, "Yeah, soldier, don't worry about it; we're up here, and we're in good shape; you don't have to worry about it." My response was, "Oh, I just don't believe nothing this heavy can stay up in the sky; it seems pretty heavy to me!" He repeated, "Don't worry about it; you see those big engines out there? They purr like a kitten." I replied, "Yeah, they may purr like a kitten, but cats die sometimes!" With that, he burst out laughing.

At this point in the flight, the pilots had put the jet on automatic pilot. Of course, I did not know anything about automatic pilot. When I looked and saw all of the pilots coming down the aisle with their hats on, shaking everybody's hands, I jumped up and shouted, "Hey! Aren't y'all suppose to be driving this thing?" One pilot said, "Yeah!" Then I asked, "What are y'all doing back here shaking everybody's hand when y'all are not driving this thing? Y'all are going to crash this thing, aren't you? Y'all have already got it overloaded!" One pilot asked if I had ever heard of automatic pilot, and I told him I had not. Then he wanted to know if I had ever ridden in a jet before. I told him that I had, and that back in Louisiana where I was from, every jet I had seen had a pilot driving it. When I said Louisiana, his comment was, "Oh, Louisiana." I replied, "Oh, nothing! Oh, why don't you go back up front and drive this thing!" I asked him how fast did the jet go, and he said about 700 miles per hour. When he said that, I glanced to the side and saw water. I realized that we were flying low; so, I said, "Naw, man, please! Why don't you go back up front and start driving this thing?" He burst out laughing and said, "Son, don't worry about this jet; this jet is on automatic pilot; it's going by itself. You're in good hands." I replied, "Can't be! Suppose this automatic pilot doesn't automatically fly this thing?" At this point, the sergeant I had talked to earlier pulled me to the side and told me not to worry; he told me that he was going to take care of me until we got to Vietnam.

Our next stop was to be Wake Island, and we still had a distance to go. We had traveled for hours on the 16,000 mile flight to Vietnam. Some of the guys were excitedly talking; some had gone to sleep. I had gotten leery.

Finally, we arrived at Wake Island. It was dark, and the way they had things calculated, it would be daylight when we arrived in Vietnam. As we continued the flight, I was uneasy; I kept dozing off and waking up. I tried to see where I was going, but it was too dark; I could not see anything on the outside through the jetliner window.

One main thing that kept me awake was a song that I was listening to entitled "A Rainy Night in Georgia" by Brook Benton. As I listened to that song, I did finally doze off to sleep.

DESTINATION REACHED:
VIETNAM!

When I woke up, I woke up in the arms of the sergeant. I had slumped over onto him. As I woke up, I could see that it was day. I still had the sound system in my ear from having fallen asleep listening to Brook Benton. As I stirred, the sergeant asked, "Are you up, boy?" I answered that I was and asked where we were. He told me that we were in Vietnam. I sighed and asked, "What's the problem; can't we take this jetliner down?" He said, "No, we can't land! Look down there!" When I looked out the window, I saw what looked like a bunch of firecrackers and fireworks. I replied that it was nothing but fireworks. The sergeant said, "Son, those are not fireworks; they are fighting down there! That's why we cannot land this jetliner." I said, "Well, can they hit us?" He replied that we were flying fairly high and that I should not worry about anything. What I did not know at the time was that the Vietnamese were set on keeping jets from bringing more troops in.

The ground fighting continued for some time, and we were forced to stay up in the air, flying around and trying to wait until the fighting ceased so that we could land. After some time of us circling around the area, we were told that our fuel was low, and we were going to reduce our altitude. This news upset me because I had been leery all along about the jetliner, and the thought of it running out of fuel had crossed my mind. So, I got real leery and uptight about the possibility of us having to land in the middle of all that fighting down below.

Finally, the fighting stopped, and we were able to land. We landed in Bien Hoa, right outside Saigon. Before we deboarded the liner, the officers lectured us about what to look out for and so forth. While they lectured us, we sat there burning up in the winter clothes we were wearing because it was by no means cold where we were. When we finally deboarded, we were hit squarely in the face with atrocious conditions. The odor of that country, the heat, our clothing—everything was awful. It was a nasty and disgusting place to be. I was glad to land and get on solid ground, away from all the water we had been traveling over, but where we were there was nothing nice in sight.

As soon as we deboarded, we had to start stripping, taking off our socks, underwear and heavy clothing to get into lighter gear. Then we got another lecture. Officers gave us instructions about our sleeping quarters and all of that. After that, it was time to eat, but I promptly discovered that I could not eat the food. I did without for hours and ended up going to sleep without eating.

While they were serving breakfast the next morning, I had to comment on the food. I simply said, "This food is bad!" However, as time passed, I got hungry; so by lunchtime, I ate. That just goes to show that when a person is hungry, he will eat regardless of what the food is.

Once we settled in, it did not take me long to observe the racial cliques that had developed. There were a number of groups—blacks with blacks, whites with whites. There were some mixed groups with black and whites, but mostly, the groups were separated according to races. I also noticed the unique handshake that the blacks used with each other. Basically, it seemed as if all the different groups—the whites, blacks and Puerto Ricans were trying to get along because we were all from the United States.

At this point and time, our biggest problem was trying to adjust to the environment, especially the heat. It took us two weeks to get used to the stifling heat and humidity. In addition to that, it was a big problem getting accustomed to how the Vietnam people lived. Their habits were so different from anything I had ever been around. They would urinate in front of everybody; they would take a crap in front of people, too, even women. These people would just pull their clothes down, do their business and go on as usual. As I saw all this, I was thoroughly confused. I did not know what was going on. I commented about how everything was so different and upsetting to me, and the guy I spoke to told me that I would get used to it. I told him that I could not see myself getting used to all of that. His response to me was to tell me to look at all the water we had crossed to get to Vietnam and if I thought I could swim back to the States I should try it. I told him that I could not swim, which was a big surprise to him. He could not understand how I had received all the training that I had received and had not been taught to swim. I told him that I had not been taught how to swim, and besides that, I was afraid of water anyhow.

After seeing all the cruddy ways the Vietnam people lived and talking to my fellow soldiers, I made up my mind that I had to adjust; I had to eat and had to live; so I had to tough it out over there, but believe me, it wasn't easy because their ways were so strange and peculiar—so, so different from ours.

In addition to crapping wherever they wanted to, they also burned their crap, and when the wind blew in a certain direction, that scent would hit me dead in the face, and that stuff stank really, really bad. I thought back to when we first deboarded the jetliner and realized that this was why the country stank. They burned their shit! I couldn't understand why they didn't just go to the bathroom or something, why they didn't at least bury it. That way they wouldn't have to burn it, and wouldn't stink up the whole country.

As we stayed in the area, I continued to see weird stuff. Once there was a boy son and a girl son playing together in a puddle of water. Boy son urinated on girl son, and nothing was done about it. I didn't understand why papa son didn't stop that from happening before we even got there. I was disgusted with the whole thing. I felt that those folks knew we were over there fighting for them. They knew that we were coming, and I figured that they should have stopped the weird behavior out of respect for those of us who weren't accustomed to their ways and were in their country fighting for them. There may not be much logic in what I thought, but that's how I thought.

After a while, I was told that I was going to the 101st Airborne Division. Once I settled in there, I noticed the racial stuff again, the little static that existed between the blacks and whites. I never got involved, but there was definitely some tension between the groups. As I mentioned earlier, the blacks had an amount to the usual handshake. Shaking hands with a brother took about 30 minutes. There was a flip, flop, flip, flop and so on for some time. I grew impatient with so much handshaking and asked them how long we were going to shake hands. I had trouble figuring out their drawn out handshake. It was like mathematics, and I never liked arithmetic. It seemed to me that their goal was to teach this complicated hand shake to every new brother who came over.

While the brothers had their handshake, the white boys had their peace sign. As I saw it, something was wrong because when I left America, people just shook hands, and that was it.

At this point, I was now located in the MAI Cong Delta, the southern part of South Vietnam. Again, I saw things I had never seen before. I had never seen so many people riding bikes. It was amazing to me how they could ride a bike with their long clothing on. I couldn't figure out how their clothing didn't get caught up in the spokes of the bike. Another thing that I observed was that most of the Vietnamese people chewed some kind of tobacco or something that made their teeth black. At first, I thought that their teeth were rotten. I later understood that the stuff they were chewing actually kept their teeth healthy. They also smoked some kind of strongly scented cigarette that one could smell standing ten feet away from them. And they drank some sort of strange beer. I tried a can of the beer once, but I just couldn't tolerate it. I realized that all of these weird customs and things were simply a part of those people's culture.

I had come from a little country town, so it wasn't that I was accustomed to everything being modern and fancy and all of that, but being in Vietnam was like we had gone back in time from the 20th Century to the 19th Century.

As I compared their way of living to what I was accustomed to, I wondered which was right and which was wrong. I finally came to the realization that they were right, and we were right because we were all behaving according to our way of standard way of life. I also learned that a lot what they did, even though it was disgusting to me, was healthy for them. The way they prepared their food, not cooking it well and to certain temperatures the way we did in the United States, did not negatively affect them. They're not taking baths and keeping their bodies clean according to American standards worked for them because this was what they were use to. I wondered how they could fight so hard and survive as well as they did with their dietary habits and lack of proper sanitation. Then it finally registered in my mind that they could do so well because they were from Vietnam, their own territory, whereas I was not. It was hard for me to survive because my Louisiana background was so very different from theirs.

When I thought back to those people being able to eat and digest cats and dogs and not being sick to their stomachs, it hit me hard that I had to get out of there. I just knew I had to get out of Vietnam! That is why I tried so hard to perfect myself on my own even though I had combat training back in the United States. I knew I had to do something to get out of there! In my mind, I asked myself how in the world I was going to get out. Then an inner voice said, "Stick with the military food." That wasn't much of comfort to me because the military food was no good either, but at least it was in cans, sealed, clean and safe. I knew it was safe so I went ahead and ate it. Eventually, believe it or not, I began to like it because I convinced my brain that food was the food for me because it came from America and not from Vietnam. I stuck with the canned goods even though the Vietnamese could cook a dog and make it smell like a rib eye or T-bone steak!

A lot of American soldiers did not stick with the military food; that's why so many of them ended up with hepatitis. They ate the Vietnamese food, but unfortunately, they did not know what they were eating when they went into the Vietnam villages.

I am convinced that a lot of the dogs that were in Vietnam that ended up missing were stolen. I can't prove it, but I am sure those dogs were stolen when the village people would come in and clean up the beds while we were away. I believe that the dogs that the American soldiers had originally were the same dogs sold back to them in the meals that they bought from the Vietnamese. Again, that is why I never ate the Vietnamese food even though many of my comrades did, and I have no doubt that they ended up eating their own dogs—and cats, too, for that matter.

I couldn't trust their food, but I will say that the Vietnamese did a good job of sewing, making up beds, making shoes out of old tires and just coming up with ways to make it—to survive. This just showed me that when people are poor; I mean really poor, they will do almost anything to survive. I could see that and understand that, but I still could not see how they could do what they did with animals and eat them.

Another thing that amazed me was how they made their hootches, their houses. They made them out of mud, straws and things like that. It puzzled me how they could live in them when the monsoon season set in because during the monsoon season, it would rain for six months straight. I couldn't understand why those hootches didn't collapse. I used to scratch my head and try to figure out why the roofs of the hootches didn't fall in. I finally asked one papa son why the hootches did not collapse, that particular papa son could not answer me because he could not speak English. So I asked if anybody there could speak English because usually in every bunch there would be at least one who could speak our language. Sure enough, there was one guy who spoke English, and he explained that the hootches did not collapse due to how they mixed the mud along with the straws. He explained that no matter how much it rained; it would not rain inside the hootches. I asked him if I could go inside after I asked him if there was anybody inside who would shoot me. He gave me permission to go inside, and as he said, the hootch was dry even though it was raining. I found that to be some strange stuff.

A family consisting of a papa son, a mama son, and a girl son were sitting peacefully inside by a fire. However, the odor in there made me quickly make my exit. Plus, I was convinced that the water would penetrate the mud and make the roof collapse.

As I left the hootch, I was still trying to figure out why the roofs didn't collapse. I did not completely buy into what the guy had said about it simply being a matter of how they mixed the straw and mud together. I finally came to the conclusion that the roofs did not collapse because the fire inside was continually drying the mud which kept the roof strong and in place. I put all this together in my head. Then I wondered how it was that the family could stand the heat. Then it quickly occurred to me that the average temperature over there was 130 degrees, so they could easily tolerate the heat.

As I traveled farther into Vietnam, I got to Phu Bai. I noticed that it was really bad up north. In the north, the Vietnamese—the Viet Cong, as they were called—seemed to be a bit smarter than the Vietnamese in the south, and the American people seemed to be a bit more cautious there, also.

When we got to Phu Bai, they kept us inside the perimeter that first night. The next morning the Hueys—the choppers—came and picked us up and took us out into the field. When we first got off the chopper, I was very scared. My mind went back to that old, hard training Drill Sergeant Stokes had taught me. I started thinking about my father and mother, and I wanted to cry, but I could not. There was an older white man that walked up to me and said, "Son, you look like you're worried." I said, "Yes, I am." Then he replied, "I will stick with you and help you remember everything that you were trained to do." About half an hour later, we made contact (fighting) which was quite severe. I started crying and tried to get up and run, but the white guy held me down and told me to get control of myself. I said, "Yes, but I just want to go home!" He hit me and said, "Take this gun and start fighting, boy! Get your ass together," he replied. He said, "Come on, boy! Come on, asshole!" I looked around at him with my body as flat to the ground as I could get it. I told him, "I will fight you if you call me a boy or an asshole again!" then he said, "That's right, fight! Hold that gun over your head and pull the trigger!" And that's what I did, and from that day, I was on my way. It seems as if God had sent someone to help me get started.

The fighting was so severe because we were near the DMZ (Demilitarized Zone). As we fought there for quite some time, I noticed and caught myself thinking that I was just killing up people, and as I did it, it seemed as though I was getting pleasure out of it, getting a kind of happy feeling about it. I finally came to the realization that this wasn't me. This wasn't the real Clabon Jones. After a while I concluded, though, that in order to survive in a war, I had to do whatever was necessary to protect myself. In a manner of speaking, the killing was like driving a car. When a person first starts driving, he is slow and cautious. Then, after he has driving for a while, he gets relaxed and happy under the wheel, and starts driving faster. He gets comfortable with the car. That's exactly how I got with my gun. I got where I could shoot to kill and not think about it.

On one particular day during the monsoon season, it was raining but still extremely hot. The Viet Cong were out in the jungles hunting and waiting for us just like we were hunting and waiting for them. It was like the first day of hunting season, and the rabbits knew it. We got into a bad firefight. Luckily, none of our men got hurt, but we killed about fifteen or sixteen Viet Cong. The main thing we had to worry about when we were fighting like that was the snipers that would be in trees. That was why the military sprayed the trees with Agent Orange to kill them and get rid of the snipers' hiding spots. However, sometimes the military made mistakes and sprayed Agent Orange on us, also. And this is why some of us came out of the Army with Post Traumatic Syndrome and Agent Orange.

During this particular day's firefighting, we had to pick the Viet Cong out of the trees, out of the ground and from on top of the ground. We had our work cut out for us. As we fought them sternly, it began to bother me that we had to keep picking up dead bodies, looking at bodies and kicking dead bodies over. It got to be a really tragic scene.

One other thing that got to me was that as soon as we walked away from one activity, we would walk right into another one and would have to start fighting again. We would be tired, running low on ammunition, food, and calories. We would run low on everything. Yet, we had to fight another bunch of them; it seemed like we had to fight group after group after group after group.

In this one particular firefight that I am looking at in my head now, we lost five men. We had to call in the ships and stop the fighting for a little while because our officers knew that we were running out of ammunition due to all of the previous fighting. Nevertheless, we had to keep moving. They finally called in a shanook. They had to land that thing down there and drop us some ammunition. Just imagine if they had dropped it to the wrong people. All they had to do was get the wrong grid coordinates. One mistake and the enemy would have gotten the ammunition and used it against us because they had American weapons that they got when they captured American soldiers. In fact, they were already using our weapons, our M-16's, our M-14's and 79's. If our men had mistakenly dropped the ammunition to them, we would have had to run from our own ammunition and guns!

After a while, we ran into a regiment of NVA's—North Vietnam Army troops. I don't know how many of them there were, but we had to steadily fight them, and those people were hard. They were very hard to put down—to kill. I remember one time when I got so mad. I actually got up—stood up—and started firing them up. I just took over for a while even though a sergeant and lieutenant were there. I got to the point that I was tired of fighting, and I just reacted that way. Those people would fight until the very end, so I got up and started firing. I told a guy on the tank to put some 155 on them; that tanks round. I soon ducked back down, though, because those bullets were flying all over the place. Luckily, I didn't get hit then and there.

However, as the fighting continued, I finally did get hit. At first, I did not know I was hit. All I knew was that I was wallowing on the ground in pain but still fighting. The NVA's would come up, and I would try to pop shoot and get them all. I was trying to kill as many as I could so that the fighting could stop, and we could go on our business. After a while, I realized that I had been hit. I felt something soggy on me, real soggy on me. I kept rubbing to the side of me; I knew I was sweating, but I didn't think I was sweating that badly. Something told me to look back, and when I did, I discovered that I was hit, and blood was coming out of my body. I had been hit in my left side. When I saw that, I dropped my gun and rolled over. I did not know how badly I had been hit. I looked to my side, and one of my comrades asked me what was wrong. I told him that I had been hit and continued rolling on the ground. It was good that I had my helmet on so tightly; otherwise my injury would have been much worse. I looked to my side again, and another guy said, "You're hit!" I said, "Damn!" Naturally, I wondered whether I was going to die, but the guy told me that I had not been hit that badly. He tried to assure me that I was going to be all right. But I wasn't satisfied with that. I said, "Naw, you're going to have to get a ship in here; call it in!" He replied that he couldn't call a ship in right then because we were under heavy fire. I told him that he had to because I was losing blood rapidly, and they had to get me to a hospital. Despite my plea for immediate help, I had to wait until all the fighting in that activity was over.

Even after the fighting calmed down, the snipers were still out there. My people had finally called, and the ship was in, but had not landed. It was flying around because the NVA's were shooting up in the sky at the Huey—the medical ship, making it impossible for it to land. Eventually, it was able to come down. Once it did, they loaded me up and took me in.

After I got to the hospital or what they called a hospital, they patched me up. I was told that I had lost a lot of blood and that I needed to drink plenty of orange juice and eat lots of beets. Well, I liked beets so I had no problem with that.

Much to my despair and surprise, I wasn't at the hospital long before they shipped me right back into jungles. The fact is, they didn't give me a chance to get well. I was still swollen, and I wasn't happy about my situation. One guy asked if they were going to wait to send me back. I quickly replied, "Look, I don't know what these people are doing! All I want to do is let these days pass so I can get the hell out of here!"

As we kept fighting, we kept being as vicious as we could be. We got to the point that when we caught NVA's, we would take our gun and really shoot them up and pull the trigger. That's exactly what we would do because they would do American soldiers worse than that. That's why I had the attitude of "never no more," and I had another attitude, and that was that I was not going to become a prisoner of war for no country, not even my own country. I decided that I would rather fight my way out! That's when I started fighting hard as hell!

The more I fought, it seemed as though there was an odor in the air around me. It seemed like something had me all wrapped up; it looked like I could feel death. There was this questioning thought that would come as soon as I got up in mornings; "Am I going to make it?" With that odor of death in the air, I woke up lots of mornings knowing that somebody was going to die, that there was going to be contact; there was going to be serious fighting. I didn't know how intense it was going to be or how mild it would be. The fact is that none of the action was mild when I had thousands and thousands of rounds coming at me a dime a dozen from on top of the ground, from underneath the ground and from out of the sky. Speaking for myself (I can't speak for the other soldiers) every day I woke up was like death day; I could smell it. I had fought so much, had done so much killing and murdering! I had done so many things that I never thought I could do in my whole life. It was awful; it was nerve-racking.

Each day presented a new set of challenges. Even on the days when we were not under fire, I would wake up after what little sleep I managed to get and not know what to expect. I didn't know if there would be a sniper with a gun on me or if we were going to run into a regiment of NVA's or if I was going to see a buddy get blown away. I didn't know anything. Every second, every minute, every hour and every quarter of an hour stood for itself!

As I continue to think back on the fighting, I can recall another firefight that was very severe. We were in Hooey. The NVA's had tanks shooting those 155 rounds. The fighting was so heavy until we had to call in the ships, as usual. The Viet Cong had come out of Laos and Cambodia. They had whipped up on the Cambodians badly. During this fight, we were fighting China men. I did not know at the time that the NVA's were coming out of China.

Later, I did notice that the NVA's that came from China were big people; they were not small like the average Vietnamese. And believe me, the NVA's were some fighting people. When we fought them, we had to really pull our triggers, we had to pull them hard. We had to really get down and fight those people because they were tough and would not give up. Besides that, a lot of them were high on opium and would still come at a person even with half of their brains shot out. The opium kept their bodies going, and seeing stuff like that was almost frightening enough to make me drop my gun and run because a lot of the time their hands would still be on their triggers. Their opium induced strength was unbelievable and scary.

Another amazing thing about these people was their commitment and loyalty to each other. I remember the time they had crossed our perimeter (the barbed-wire fence we had put up to keep them out), and I was on the ground shooting them up as fast as I could as they tried to cross; I mean I was firing them up, but the first one that got shot had the courage and the fortitude before he died to lie across the barbed-wire fence so that the others could trample over him to get to us. They were like yellow jackets, a group of bees; they had that kind of respect and unity. We would be killing up practically all of them, and the guys behind a shot guy would run over his stomach or his back, depending on which way he fell, to get to us Americans.

When they did manage to cross our perimeter, that's when the Claymore Mines came in handy. We had those so that we could just push a button, blow them up and kill them before they could get to us. As I said previously, these NVA's were tough fighters. So, some of them were able to cross our perimeter even though we had sophisticated weapons. The fact was that they had sophisticated weapons, too. Luckily, we had more weapons than they had, and we had Cobras (jets) in the sky.

Sometimes, I had to crawl backward because the enemy got so close to me. They were so aggressive until we had to also use flame-throwers. Those flame-throwers would stop them because fire will stop anything, believe me!

Another weapon we had at our disposal was the Law. The Law was one weapon that a person really had to be careful dealing with, especially standing behind it because it was powerful. The backfire of the Law was as bad as the front fire, as I mentioned before. The M79 was another powerful weapon we had. When I was humping (shooting) the M79, I would try to shoot a NVA directly in the chest because it would blow him up, and I figured that the bones and fragments from the explosion would probably hit and kill another NVA running or crawling nearby. I figured that the bone fragment might hit another one of them in the throat or in the eye, and that we could get closer, shoot them up and kill them. We wanted to get close enough to put the gun in their mouths, shoot them up, get rid of them and carry on.

As we went on and on and on, there were so many firefights, so much anger. Anger was between the North Vietnam and the South Vietnam troops because often times we had South Vietnam troops with us. They were with us because we did not know the territory; we did not know that part of the jungle. I am assuming that before I got to the area, the military had trained the South Vietnam troops so that they could train us how to go into that jungle.

They had what was known as the Ho Chi Minh Trail. We had to go down that trail, and, buddy, there was no playing there! We had to stop them from bringing ammunition from the North to the South. We ran into so much action on Ho Chi Minh Trail! We had to start killing them up like crazy; it was massive. We had to try and dismantle them. Don't get me wrong; it was not an easy job! They were some hard troops, and they were very well equipped. It was not only the North Vietnam troops and the troops from China, but there were also Laotians troops and some others that I couldn't even recognize what they were. I did not see any Russian troops, however. All of the different troops were brown-skinned so none of them looked Russian. Personally, I did not care what they were! I just knew that if they were humping their guns, and we were all looking for each other, we had to get rid of them first.

I remember one incident when we were in the jungle getting sniped on, and one of our men got shot and killed. We could not figure out where the sniper was; we simply couldn't figure it out. We looked and looked and looked, and finally we had a breakthrough due to a mistake the sniper made. He was up in a tree, and he had a watch on. I was walking past at that particular time, and I spotted him when my eye caught a glare from the sun's reflection on his watch. He was hidden in the tree and was trying to pick us off one by one. I gave a hand signal for one of the soldiers to give me the Law. I mounted the Law, and at that time, nobody knew what I was doing. However, I kept my eyes on the glare from the watch, and when I saw the sniper, I pulled up the clip; aimed real well and blew him clean out of the tree and blew half the tree away, also. I was very cautious, not knowing what else to expect. Sure enough, there were some other troops in the background, a distance from us. We went about fifteen clicks (miles) and sneaked up on them. They were eating rice from some kind of little bag that they carried it in. They were talking—yang yang yang this and yang yang yang that. I had no idea what they were saying. I concluded that they were expecting us to be breaking down for the night, but the fact was that we had surprised them. I gave the hand signal indicating that we had to get rid of them. We surrounded them in a triangle formation and shot them up. We threw some of them in holes; we left some on top of the ground. We took the time to search some of them, but we were careful to keep some of our soldiers on the look-out because we did not know if there were another regiment of them farther down the line coming towards us or not.

As I searched the dead and reflected on all the stuff that we were doing, I always thought in the back of my head, "This is bad! This is bad! What we are doing is bad on both sides!" There were times when I would think like that, but I realized I could not dwell on those kinds of thoughts because then I would stop concentrating on what I was supposed to do, and the enemy would have a chance to look down on me and say, "This is bad!" No matter what; I realized that I had to maintain.

Shortly after this action, we moved on and came to a village. Our interpreter asked some people in one of the hootches that we came to if any Viet Cong or NVA's had been there. We were told no, but that was a lie because while some of us were inside the hootch questioning them, some of us were on the outside, and the biggest firefight ever broke out. Children were in the way; mama son and papa son were in the way, but we started firing because we suspected that something was wrong, and we didn't know who was hiding in the hootch. We started firing. Finally, they retreated, but by the time they retreated, we had killed about twenty of them.

Usually, we would just drag the dead Vietnamese out and line them up. However, we made our business to be more harsh with the NVA's. They were such fierce fighters against us until we would unload a whole magazine (clip) on them to make sure those suckers were dead.

As we traveled farther North toward De Nang and Hue, we got into a lot more firefights. Some of our fights were with the regular Vietnamese troops, not just the NVA's. When we fought them, we would really kill them up because they weren't any competition for us. They were not very skilled and did not have topnotch training. They were not skilled at shooting or killing, and they did not know the little technicalities. A perfect example of their lack of skill and finesse was that sniper in the tree wearing a watch that gave off a glare which allowed me to bring him down. It was obvious to me that the regular Vietnamese were quite different from the NVA's. As I said before, the NVA's did not only had

77

the Chinese, but they also had the North Koreans troops helping them. That gave them an advantage, and we had to deal with all of them.

One night we were packed heavy and headed toward De Nang. We were going up the line to De Nang, and when we got there, we were pinned down and could not do anything. I did not know that we had orders to go into Cambodia, but I discovered later that things were happening the way they were at this time because of President Nixon. He had decided to send American troops into Cambodia. We did not know what Nixon had decided, but we were traveling north. Another thing we discovered as we got into firefights with the NVA's in that area was that they had very sophisticated weapons—Russian weapons. We thought that they would be fighting with little pop guns, but that was definitely not the case.

The NVA's that we were fighting in De Nang were small people. Yet, the Russian guns that they were humping were big. Seeing them humping those weapons reminded me of an ant because an ant can carry about three times its weight. Usually, I could see the gun before I could see them because they were so little. I was amazed that they were strong enough to carry such heavy guns when all they ate was one meal a day, and it was rice.

Of all the Viet Cong and NVA's we shot and killed, the only food we ever found on them was rice. It was puzzling to me how those folk could eat so little, carry all those heavy guns and still fight the hell out of us! The fact was they were just that tough!

As for us Americans, we were running low on food, and we were getting weaker and weaker. As we moved farther north toward the Demilitarized Zone, my survivor's instincts kicked in, and I made up my mind that I was going to eat any and all food that anybody threw away. I knew that if we ran out of food there in the jungle, we would be too weak to fight. So my plan was to fortify myself for the fighting that I knew was coming.

Just as I had figured, we got into severe fighting that lasted about five hours. The enemy was popping up on us from the back, the front, the sides—everywhere! I was crawling on the ground, and at that particular time, I was humping the M-60. We were engaged in some serious shooting, and I could not hear. So I had to rely on my eyes to look all around me so that I didn't get run over by the tracks and tanks like one of my comrades did (I saw this tank run dead over him, and blood splashed everywhere). Besides watching out for tracks and tanks running over me, I had to watch out for my own men shooting me because sometimes the guys riding on top of the tanks would make mistakes. The tanks were big and high from the ground so some of our men crawling around on the ground got accidentally run over by our own tanks.

In all of that action, things were tense. I had to keep my wits about me. I had to be super observant. Not only did I have to watch out for the tanks and my own people shooting me, but I had to watch out for the greeno, the new guy, who was likely to go crazy and start shooting everything in sight, not meaning to, but just because he had never seen anything like that before. The fact is there was a multitude of dangers I had to dodge—the greeno, jets—Phantoms and Cobras—in the sky. I had to make sure we had the right grid coordinates to shoot them because usually they wouldn't be too many clicks from us. And I had to watch out for the enemy who was definitely out to get us. In other words, I had to watch out for everything; I had to watch out for my life!

At the end of this particular action, we had killed about twenty-five men. Some of the enemy who were shot were still alive but in really bad shape, so we had to go ahead and take them out because we still had some humanity and didn't like to see people suffer. In some cases, I was not ordered to do some of the things I did; I just made decisions that it was what had to be done in order for us to continue onward, and I did them. I had made up my mind that if somebody was out to get me, I was going to get him first. I simply had to do my job as an infantryman. As I said before, after a while, I got used to the killing.

We continued farther and farther up north until we got to Hue. In Hue, we were near the Demilitarized Zone, and extremely heavy fighting started. We were so tired until we had stopped picking up dead bodies; we decided we would just let them lay wherever they fell, and if they weren't dead and were still kicking, we would just let them kick. We were tired of fighting; we were exhausted! However, we had to be careful because some of the ones kicking would be faking and would get back up and shoot us. The fact was, a lot of those guys were on opium, cocaine, weed, and all kinds of drugs which made them almost indestructible. I developed the habit of walking backward from a firefight so that if anybody moved I could shoot. If I had to shoot anybody a second time, I made sure he was dead because I would unload a whole clip on him. As I saw it, once he was dead, then he would be out of his misery.

HEADED FOR CAMBODIA

At this point, we were near the DMZ, as I said earlier, and our captain had gotten a call that we were supposed to invade Cambodia. We had already passed the Black Virgin Mountains which was where we needed to be, so we had to turn and go back. We traveled back one night, and when we got back, we realized that we were in Chulai, and there was a big time fighting there. I mean, those people did not let up! We got involved in that fighting even thought we did not know exactly what was going on. We were steadily fighting them as hard as we could. They were losing men, and we were losing men. The scene was horrendous! Men's heads were burst open by all the rounds—the AK-47's, the M-16's! It seems like everybody was getting shot up. We were battling it out! We had the Law; they had the AK-47's. We were all pounding it out there.

The enemy was tough, but we were tough, too. The 101st Airborne Division was a very proud and hard fighting unit. In fact, we were one of the hardest fighting units in Vietnam; few of the other units could match up with 101st Division. We had to show the enemy that if they crossed the line, they would die. Of course, they crossed, so we were constantly fighting, fighting and fighting. They would retreat every once in a while, but they always had a sniper somewhere around. That meant that we always had to keep an eye out for them.

When the fighting slowed down a bit, I said to the captain, "Look, I'm getting tired of this; it's too much fighting! When are we going to go back down south?" to me, down south was a little bit quieter, and I could think because the farther we got north to the DMZ, the worse the things were because there was action all day and all night, and we had to constantly be on our P's and Q's. The captain answered me with, "Look, we don't have time to talk right now!" I responded with, "No, I'm not going to stay right here; I want to know what's going on! When are we going to retreat back down south?" He answered with, "I'll tell you what, we just got orders that we have to go into Cambodia." Then I knew that the Ho Chi Minh Trail ran out of Laos through Cambodia and that was how the Vietnamese got their ammunition shipped all the way down south. It was like a road going from California to New York, and we had to head them off. After the captain told me this, I got mad and said, "Look, if we've got to go into Cambodia after all this fighting we have already done, we're not going to make it. We are not going to survive!" He replied, "Your MOS is 11B10; you are infantry, and this is what you are going to do. You came here to fight airborne, and you're going to fight!" There was nothing that I could say in response to him because what he said was true.

As we got farther down South, there was so much fighting until we could not sleep. Our situation was bad; we were tired, hungry and just plain miserable. We had to put up with leeches and water buffaloes, and crazy guys on drugs who were likely to get up in the middle of the night to take a urine, crack a stick on the ground with their foot and start shooting, putting us into another firefight. As weird as it may sound, there were actual times when we ended up in firefights (losing more men) because one man on drugs decided he wanted to get up and do what he wanted to do.

Because of situations like those and because I knew that we were going into Cambodia, I decided that I wanted to talk to the major when we got back to our base.

In selecting my men, I wanted the guys that had clear heads and weren't likely to make too many mistakes. I didn't want the ones on drugs or alcohol. Actually, I did not worry about the ones on alcohol because I knew that I could work the alcohol out of their system within four hours. My concern was about the ones on drugs, shooting up and smoking weed. I could not accept them. Unsurprisingly, I got into trouble because I rejected some guys. Some threatened me and accused me of not liking them. I had some tell me that they thought I was supposed to be a "brother," and my reply to that was that I was a "brother" to everyone as long as everybody did his job so that we could all get back home.

Brother, Soul Man, White Boy, Black Boy—it didn't matter to me who they were or what they called themselves as long as they did their jobs and did them right. I didn't want anybody out in the fields stepping on land mines, making mistakes firing at a water buffalo and letting the enemy know our location so that they could sneak up and kill us. I could not afford to have anybody out there drugging or doing anything except what he was supposed to be doing so that we could all come out of there.

As I worked with my crew of men, for some reason, I had a lot of problems with some of the guys from up North. I hate to say it, but it seems like some of those guys were not disciplined young men. Some of them were drug addicts from the start. Simply put, some of them were undisciplined, rambunctious young guys. They were unlike most of the guys from the South who were disciplined and followed orders well. In actuality, there weren't many guys from the South who were on drugs.

Yes, I had a lot of complications with some of the guys from up North. I really had some rough times with those guys.

I soon found out that discipline wasn't the only problem with some of those guys from up North. They were quick to jump to conclusions, and they thought that they knew everything. They would halfway listen to orders and then act on what they half-heard. Then after they made a mistake, they wanted everybody else to bail them out. It was obvious that the guys from the South had much better common sense, home training and parental guidance; they were much easier to command and work with. Even the guys from the big cities in the South like New Orleans had better discipline and behavior than those guys from the East or West Coast. It seemed like those guys had little or no parental guidance in their homes. Some of them were like loose cannons.

The city boys made mistakes because they did not know much about outdoors—the woods and such. Those of us from the South were the ones who were used to hunting rabbits, shooting squirrels, and looking for frogs in the woods of Louisiana, Mississippi, Alabama, Georgia and other southern states. We knew a little more about the woodlands which were similar to the jungles that we had to deal with in Vietnam. On the other hand, there was a lot of common sense, practical stuff that the city boys did not know. They thought they knew, and they thought they knew us country guys, but those city boys made some very wrong judgments about us country boys; they had no idea what we country boys knew. They had to be trained about everything; whereas, we southern guys were practically trained already. We knew how to run from Blue runner snakes. We knew how to shoot birds, squirrels, rabbits and do all kind of things. We definitely had the upper hand.

Even though I had to deal with all of these different type guys as a part of my crew, it didn't stop me. When we got out in the field, we all had to do whatever we could to survive. It's a shame to say, but there were times when grown men would holler and cry out for their mothers and fathers during firefights (I say grown men, most of us were only 18 or 19 years old; there were a few older guys who may have been 20 years old). I even cried for my mama a few times myself before I got broken in.

Out there in the fields, I had a lot of responsibility; I had to keep my guys down as they crawled around on the ground so they wouldn't get shot. I did my best to keep as many of them alive as possible because we needed all the manpower we could muster during firefights when bullets would be flashing and ricocheting everywhere.

Also, as a sergeant in charge of a crew, I had to deal with the new guys, and of course, I had problems with them. Then there were the ones I called the mediums—those who had been out in the fields two or three months and knew the ropes a little but not too much. And then there were the seasoned guys like myself who had been around for some time and knew almost everything and had the added duty of having to train and try and save the others. It just goes to show how things turn out. People had trained and taught me when I first got to Vietnam, and I ended up having to train other guys. It turned out to be a chain reaction type situation with everybody looking out for everybody else.

Where there had been race issues among the troops before, during all the battles and firefights, everybody realized that we all had to work together to cover each other's back. Color and where a person was from meant absolutely nothing! Believe me, color was not the big issue at the time because our lives came first! I mean, when it came down to fighting, color wasn't on anybody's mind. Even the most prejudiced, rednecks from Alabama, Louisiana and other areas, dropped the race thing while we were out in the fields fighting for our lives. That just goes to show that this racial stuff that we have in the United States is just a game that people play and a dangerous game at that! Over in Vietnam we had to be brothers whether a person was Puerto Rican, Honduran, White,

Black, Mexican, or whatever. We had to hang together, be together, do everything together—we had to work together! That's why I know that the people of the United States can work better together than we do now. It's just selfishness that keeps us from doing so.

The military action was consistent the whole time that we were in De Nang, Hue and those areas. Before we started to move back down south, we encountered NVA's once again, and we fought and fought with them. As I previously stated, those NVA's were well equipped and well trained. They had been trained by Russians, North Koreans, and Chinese troops. The Viet Cong, on the other hand, had not received such good training. They had gotten a little training from the North Vietnamese and then had been sent out to the fields with guns to fight. NVA's were comparable to use American troops. The Viet Cong basically only knew how to break a gun down, load it and shoot.

Because the NVA's were so well trained, they were very aggressive. So, we had to get down and deal with them. What I mean deal with them is that we had to have our heads screwed on right to fight those people; we couldn't just knick, knack with them. We had to call in Cobra's jets, and we had to get down, dig in and really fight them. During the particular firefight that I am currently thinking of, I don't know exactly how many, but the NVA's lost a lot of men because we called the Cobras and the Fathoms on them. Fortunately for us, we only lost two men, but the fight was fierce.

I recall one white guy from Missouri who asked me, "Do you believe that we are going to make it out of here?" I said, "I don't know; we're headed back down south. We've just got to battle our way down. I don't know why we went back up north; now we've got to battle it back down south." I thought that once we battled our way north, fighting the troops as hard as we had to get there, that they would at least bring in ships, helicopters and Hueys to take us out of there. However, that was not the case, we had to go back down the same trail that we had traveled to get north. The problem was that we were worn out, tired, hungry and running out of ammunition. Imagine us needing 100 pounds of ammunition to fight out way to the north and then needing another 100 pounds to fight our way back south following the same path yet having only 10 pounds of the 100 pounds that we needed. That's precisely the position that we were in, and that's what scared me the most at the time.

While I was pondering the situation that we were facing, the guy from Missouri made an observation. He said that he had been noticing me and how tough I talked to my men. He said that the men had loaded guns and could easily get rid of me. I responded with, "I pick my men; I picked you. I picked who I wanted to go out into the field with me. I noticed you before you noticed me. I noticed that you weren't on drugs, smoking pot, sniffing cocaine—none of that. That's why I picked you. We are going to make it. I have a good group here." Luckily, I did have a good group; however, there were so many guys out in the fields who were thoroughly confused because they were young, scared, inexperienced and had never been in a war before.

As I continued to talk to the Missouri guy, we moved southward into the jungles and into more firefights. Unfortunately, we lost this guy. He got hit in the head, and there was nothing that I could do. This was just one of the many times I would see friends shot in the head, the chest, the heart or wherever, and there was virtually nothing that I could do as they kicked, grasped for air and suffered there on the ground near me. My position was that I had to maintain my composure, focus on the fighting and go on with what I was trained for and what I had learned out there in the jungles. During times like those, it was apparent to me why it was so important that we had learned everything possible. Why they drilled us so hard and why the drill sergeants had been so rough on us in basic training.

Because of my training and conditioning, I knew that I couldn't stop and feel sorry for a wounded friend or comrade in the middle of a firefight. Of course, after the firefight, if a comrade was still alive, kicking and in deep distress with half of his face shot off or his chest blown out or wounded to the point that I knew he wasn't going to make it, I would resort to the training that we all had, I would use comforting to take him out of his misery.

Telling about what I had to do in those kinds of situations is not a pleasant thing to do, and it's horrible to think about some of the things I have had to do in my life. Yet, those things happened—those things and more. Some I choose to write about and some I cannot.

During another firefight, one of my other buddies got hit. He got hit in the shoulder. I have forgotten his name; yet, I can see his face in my head. When he got shot, he rolled over to me and said that he was burning up. I told him that I knew he was because bullets are hot. I told him to just stay put and keep his head down. I told him not to roll over anymore but to stay still. He was hollering and hollering and asking me if he was going to make it. I told him that he was just hit in the shoulder and not to worry about it. He said that he was worried about his main artery. I told him that he was bleeding pretty badly, but I thought that he was going to make it because he was very strong. I admonished him to keep still while I cut a strip from the old jungle shirt I had on and stuffed it in his wound. It took me a while to do this because we were in the head of battle; I had to locate my pocketknife, and the fighting was very intense.

The reader may recall that in a previous incident when I wrote about when the Missouri guy got hit, I just watched as he expired and did nothing to help. Yet, with this particular situation, I helped. The question may come to mind as to why I didn't help one but helped the other. Well, the fact is, the first guy got shot in the head; the second guy was hit in the shoulder, which was a big difference. There was hope for the second guy. Not only that, his body was on fire from the bullet because those bullets were super hot and burned badly. In this case, I had to stop and stuff his would with my shirt to give him some relief because I knew he had a good chance of making it.

In the midst of trying to help him, I still had to watch out for myself because I could hear the bullets zooming by my head. One wrong move of my head and I would have gotten hit. I managed to stuff his wound and tie him up somewhat. He got quieter as I held him in my arm, but it was hard shooting an M-16 with one hand. Ordinarily an M-16 is easy, much easier to shoot than an M-14, but it wasn't easy shooting with one hand while trying to hold him down because he was burning up. Yet, I knew that I had to keep him down or he would have been shot again. Finally, he did calm down.

As we continued fighting, it seems like the North Vietnamese troops got impatient and wanted to move in more forcefully on us. That's when I gave the signal for our men to throw everything they had on them. They started coming over the perimeter, but my strategy was to keep some grenades and some extra rounds of ammunition in case we had to blow our way out of that particular area.

At this point, we were in the process of fighting our way down from the north to the central part of Vietnam where we were going to leave from to go to Cambodia. I knew that as we traveled, we were going to run into activity after activity after activity! Activity was fighting, and I knew we would have firefight after firefight after firefight. I also knew we were going to run out of food.

In the meantime, my wounded friend got stronger, and for a short while, the fighting slowed down a little bit. My friend kept asking me if I thought he was going to die because of all the blood he had lost. I told him not to think like that, that we just had to get the ships in, and we would be okay. A short time later, the radio men came and called in a medical ship that was mounted with an M-60 on top; it was a Huey with a red cross on it. After much difficulty, it finally came in and picked my buddy up, and from what I understand, he made it.

It's strange how I would be so close to a person, helping him out, teaching him this and teaching him that and doing everything I could for him, and then he would get hit, go back home, and I would never hear from or see the person again. Consequently, I spent a lot of time thinking about people that had crossed my path.

As we steadily traveled, we got into other firefights. A little Mexican guy named Gomez got hit. He and I were not tight buddies, but we talked a lot, and I had picked him for my crew. When he got hit, I can recall what a hard time he had. I remember that he became hysterical, hollering and screaming that he wanted to go back home, and that he wasn't supposed to be in Vietnam because he was a Mexican, that the fighting was wrong, and that the U.S. wasn't going to do anything about him getting shot up like he was. And I bet that he was right; I bet that our government didn't do much of anything to help him.

I remember that as Gomez was injured and wallowing on the ground, there were four or five other guys there with him, hurt and wallowing in pain, also. Just picture, the situation that we were in, trying to take care of all those wounded soldiers and at the same time being under fire with jets flying over our heads dropping bombs and Fathoms and Cobra ships throwing bombs, too. During these firefights, we were dealing with all kinds of weapons—the Law, the flame-throwers, the M-16's—everything! It was all messed up!

As I think back on those firefights, one thing that stands out; all the little pity pat squabbles that took place among the different races—the squabbles among the Blacks, Whites, Mexicans, Hondurans and Puerto Ricans—all ceased. We all became one big family; I mean one big family depending on each other out there in the fields. I have often thought about this, and anyone over there who looked at our situation could see it. There had been times when everybody thought that he was such and such and this and that, but once a person got in the field and started fighting, he soon realized that we all had to become as one, and this is precisely what we did while we were in Vietnam.

As we traveled back down coming from De Nang, we got to Qui Nhon, close to Pleiju which was our base. As we got close to Pleiku, the fighting heat was heavy, and we had lost a lot of men. Fortunately, we did not have too far to go because Qui Nhon and Pleiku were only about 35 miles from each other. However, fighting through and getting back to Pleiku turned out to be a big problem because the enemy had trip wires, land mines and detonated mines waiting for us. As we went through, we did indeed hit some of those mines.

When some of our guys went off track, they accidentally ran over the mines, and when they hit the mines, I could see those guys flying up into the sky. It was a shocking thing to see bodies flying up into the sky. Those guys were our buddies; we had all become as one; we had stop worrying about crazy stuff! We just saw ourselves as one. So, scenes like those were awful. Once a bomb exploded, bodies and body parts flew into the sky, and a head, leg or torso would fall down and hit us soldiers who were shooting with our heads flat on the ground. We would be as flat to the ground as a piece of Wrigley's chewing gum, and when those body parts fell on us, many of us ended up with broken necks or backs and in some cases killed because those parts were heavy as they fell to the ground after having been blown high into the sky. Also, when those parts fell, they fell down as solid fragments that could kill a soldier dead as a door nail, crippled him pretty badly or break his back.

When bullets would hit guys lying beside me, bone fragments would hit and stick in me in the face and blood would splash into my eyes. Believe me, that stuff hurt because I was lying right there beside a guy and got the full impact. When President Kennedy got hit, I am sure Jackie Kennedy could tell us about the impact, if she were alive. Trust me, those bullets hit a human body very, very hard. So when we were fighting out there, it was dangerous in all kind of ways! A soldier could get hurt directly or indirectly from somebody else's misfortune.

There were times when the enemy found our own May Palm that some of the dumb guys left behind, and they would use that May Palm on us. If a person wants to see a human body burn and disintegrate, all he would need to see is a person hit by May Palm. That stuff would hit a person in the head, go straight through him and come out of his behind. It would eat clean through human flesh. Time and time again, I saw guys set on fire when they were hit with May Palm or with flame-throwers, and there was absolutely nothing we could do for them as they ran screaming and hollering, with their bodies completely on fire.

All kinds of tragic things happened out there in the fields. As I said previously, we were under constant pressure from the possibility of our own tracks running over us, our own men shooting us, jets flying over and throwing bombs down, us being on the ground throwing lead at the enemy and them throwing lead back at us! It was simply a chaotic situation when we were out there in those jungles. I was really blessed by the Lord that I was not killed like so many of the men I fought with, and I have much respect for them as I think back on what they endured.

By this point in our fighting, we had gone over into Cambodia. I immediately noticed that the Cambodians were very good-looking people. They had dark complexions and were medium built. I also noticed that their hootches—their homes—were high off the ground sitting on sticks. I wondered why they built them that way, and I soon discovered that their homes were built high from ground because of the cobra snakes which were so prevalent there. They had to put their homes up to escape the cobras—to survive. As I observed their living conditions, their poverty, I wondered why we were over there fighting them. They were so poor, and we had so much compared to them. I came to the conclusion that President Nixon had made a very sorry, sorry decision for us to go into Cambodia. All it did was spread the war into Cambodia and Laos. I understood that Nixon made that decision because he knew the weapons were coming from Cambodia, and we could head them off. Indeed, that was one justification for us being there, but as I saw things, our being there was wrong because it caused me to be there, and that's where I got wounded. I got blown up; my eyes got blown up, and I was seriously injured. Besides that, being in Cambodia forced us to be mixed with Cambodians, Laotians, Chinese, and Vietnamese. One can only imagine the situation that we were in, looking at those different people and all of them having swipe eyes in their heads. How were we supposed to distinguish and determine who was whom?

Since we were in such a predicament, I made the decision that I would pull my trigger first and not worry about trying to figure things out. In addition to that, we had Vietnamese who were on our side fighting with us. So, how in the devil could we distinguish who was whom over there? It was extremely difficult—too difficult. All I knew was that if they were not Americans, when I pulled that trigger I meant to slaughter them just like I had been trained to do. I did not have time to stall and wait to see who was on my side or who wasn't. What I visualized in my mind was being out in the field, seeing the enemy, hesitating to pull the trigger and knowing that I was going to die. So I knew that it was up to me to pull my trigger first! There were just too many people of Asian descent over there, looking alike, and I was forced to make the hard decisions that I had to make in order to survive.

As we traveled through Cambodia, which was a beautiful country, we encountered a lot of firefights in the jungles. We fought the Chinese with their Russian guns and Russian Migs. Also, as we traveled north toward Laos, we had many, many more firefights which resulted in a lot of deaths which caused me to do a lot of things that I did not like to do—a lot of killing. A lot of the men that were in my group, a third of the 506 101st Airborne Division in Vietnam, were fighting extremely hard. We were not getting any sleep; we weren't getting any food. We were virtually running on empty. And all of this was because at this particular time, President Nixon had called an air strike on Cambodia, Laos and Vietnam which, as I previous said before, caused the spread of the war. These facts are recorded in the books in Washington, D.C. Anyone doubting the truth of what I am recalling can sue me; Nixon was the culprit; he ordered the bombing that spread the war into Cambodia!

We fought hard in Cambodia. We were hungry; we were tired. I, personally, was tired of picking up dead bodies, and I was tired of killing them. We were all sick and tired of fighting Chinese, Laotians, North Vietnamese—everybody. My whole division, the 101st Airborne and the 125th Division were some tough fighting men, but we had run down at this point. What made it extra hard for me was that I was a point man and we were mechanized. It was our duty to go up and down the country looking for problems, looking for fighting. When I went into the military, I had no idea that I would be in a unit like that and in a place where I didn't know the people and I didn't know the terrain. I now knew that I was just a young country boy, 18 years old, fighting real hard for the United States.

Whether I have earned respect or not earned respect, everything that I have said in this book is true. It is the gruesome truth that we invaded many hootches and villages in Cambodia. We went into the villages and tore them down and shot them up. Unfortunately, there weren't just young people in those villages. There were children, babies, middle-aged people and some really old folk in them (some looked like they were 90 years old or older), and we had to shoot them up; we had to kill them!

Whether the United States likes it or not, I am telling it the way it was. We had to go into those hootches and kill up everything in them! This is exactly what the United States had us do overseas, and then they camouflaged the facts on TV and radio back in the States.

In a lot of cases, I shot around the heads of the old folk and children, pretending to kill them, and sometimes I made mistakes and did actually kill them. Yet, I tried my best not to hit them because they were older people, or they were kids. Even though I was a point man shooting and killing on a Search and Destroy Mission, and I was supposed to do just what it said: search and destroy, I just couldn't kill the children and old folk unmercifully like that.

In my mind, the ugliness of the Vietnam War is endless. I can recall the many, many battles in Vietnam and Cambodia where I saw so much blood and had so much blood splashed in my face. It seemed that at times we were swimming in blood. It was common to fight in the same bloodstained clothes for two or three weeks at a time, with the blood from as many as thirty different bodies on those clothes. Believe me, that blood stank! Blood naturally stinks. It has an odor to it once it hits the air and as it gets old. Often, we had to walk miles and miles in bloody, sweaty in those bloody clothes. Oftentimes as we roamed the jungles in those foul smelling clothes, we had our own injuries with our own blood mixed in with all the rest—and we had to carry bloody bodies! Besides that, we were constantly hungry, sleepy, tired, and anxious, with our nerves getting bad because never in our lives had we seen or experienced such horrors as those in the war fields.

As we traveled north, we were on the Hoa Che Mien Trial, and the farther north we pushed, the harder we fought. We ran into what was called Bromeans—my brothers—black guys and white guys. Everybody was brother then. We were all fighting hard and sticking together. We did not have the ignorant racial stuff that we had in the States. We had to fight; we had to stay intact because we had to fight those China men, Laotians, and the North Vietnamese or NVA's, as they were called. We had to be together; we had to stick together, we had to know our signs, we had to survive!

There was another incident where we had to fight for about five hours, and the enemy was unyielding. We called in the Cobra gunships, the Fathoms and the F-15's. We were under extreme fire. Our enemies had opium in them, and they would fight until the last because they were high on the opium and did not know what they were doing. They would run straight into a gun. It was something seriously wrong with those people; they were fearless! So, we had to shoot them up badly; we often had to unload a clip on them in order to kill them. Because we did this, we used up most of our ammunition, knowing that the Hueys wouldn't come in to drop more ammunition down to us.

My worry was whether we were going to have enough ammunition to fight our way back across the border into Vietnam to our base. I could not understand how we were going to be able to do that. It was a lame, scary, and hard fighting situation. I ended up voicing my thoughts to my lieutenant. I said, "Look, why don't we just stop fighting and try to head back because my rounds are running out! I only have four grenades on me in my pockets. Why don't we just head back?" He replied that I was there because I was obeying orders. I answered him with, "I don't give a damn about orders; let's just get our asses back to Vietnam!" The lieutenant then said, "That's not our orders; our orders were to come to Cambodia and head off all the ammunition going to South Vietnam." In response to that, I said, "Hell yeah, but we're up north trying to head that off. They have other routes and directions. We're not from here; we don't know this territory!" He then told me that if I didn't get in my position he would have me court marshaled. I told him that I didn't care if he had me court marshaled or not; all I wanted to do was get out of there because those people knew the area. They were underground, in the air and all around everywhere, and we were at a disadvantage just as they would have been if they had gone to Baton Rouge, Louisiana where they didn't know the territory.

Finally, I came to the conclusion that our military was trying to play hardball, going strictly by orders from Washington, D.C. I decided then that I might as well go along and fight the enemy and fight them off as the best way I could.

About that time, we got into heave activity right at the Laotian border, there at the corner between Cambodia and Vietnam. I repeat; I was with a mechanized crew, and it was our job to travel and fight. As we fought, bullets often zoomed right by my head. Thanks be to God that I didn't get killed even though I did get hit in Vietnam and Cambodia.

Whenever my mind drifts back to the times I was hit, I think about how it was just good to be alive in the midst of all that havoc because I had seen so many of my comrades get shot. I knew how the bullets burned and hurt and how much these guys suffered. I realize how blessed I was because I had seen men who were shot in the leg or hand and died and others who were shot in the chest or brain and lived. I had also seen men shot in the hip who died and those who were shot in the hip and lived. I can't explain it; that was just how things happened.

What was peculiar and puzzling to me and what I couldn't understand was that I was supposed to be fighting at war in one country, and yet Uncle Sam had gotten me a long ways from home and had then ordered me to fight in another country. I accepted the fact that I had been sent to fight in Vietnam, but I did not accept the fact that I ended up someplace else. Why I ended up in Cambodia, in Laos and in the Demilitarized Zone, I do not know!

As I said before, we were running out of ammunition. The ships—the Hueys and the Shunooks—would come in and try to drop us more ammunition but could not get to us because we were under such extreme fire. A lot of times as gun ships were flying over Cambodia, trying to get to us, they would get shot down. That made it super tough for us there on the ground because without the ammunition, food and water from the ships, we were out of luck.

Eventually, the supply ships got to us, and when they did, we were almost out of everything—food, ammunition and water. Yet, we were steady fighting and killing up those folk. At some points, it looked as if the enemy was doing better than we were doing even though we had the technology. There were times when they only had one gun a piece, particularly the Vietnamese. However, the North Korean and China men were well equipped with guns, ammunition and everything they needed to fight a war. We American soldiers had everything, too, but we still had trouble fighting those Asians. Whether the United States likes it or not, the fact is those were some vicious fighting people!

I can't emphasize enough how cautious I had to be about what I did and how I did it while in Vietnam. As I mentioned earlier, a lot of the American soldiers were cracking up over there because they were involved in actions that they had never witnessed before in their lives. They had seen so much gruesome stuff until we had problems with our own men. Some of the men's nerves were shot; therefore I had to be extra careful not to set anybody off. There were times when I had to be calmed down, too, because the stress was simply too much. It was impossible for anyone to maintain calmness and composure during a war when he was being shot upon day and night. Nevertheless, in order to survive, I had to think fast, act fast, be accurate with my gun, know my signs and keep a cool head; I had to maintain.

A lot of people think that a war is like a street shooting or gang fighting, but it's not like that at all. It's a lot of headache, pain, misery, and grief. In 'Nam and in Cambodia, a personal war in what is called a Cluster F. He had to always look out for his fellowmen, as I said, because some of them were subject to get nervous and shoot whatever moved. Sometimes, they would lose their minds completely over there in the jungles. They would think that they were shooting at the enemy, but their guns were on automatic, and in a rage, they would shoot their own men. They did not mean to do so, but they were scared, nervous and out of control. Anyone who has ever been in a war can understand what they were up against, with them seeing their friends and comrades being shot and having to roll over their dead bodies as they continued to pound an enemy who was pumped up with opium and almost indestructible. It was simply too much, and some of these men had reached and gone beyond their limit. That's why they cracked.

American has been all overseas fighting in various countries, but I don't believe that America has encountered anybody as fast as the Vietnamese were. These people proved to be a ferocious enemy who were determined to fight to the very end of their being!

As I see it, the Vietnam War was one of the most destructive wars that the United States could have ever engaged in. It was the bloodiest thing that I have ever seen or could have ever imagined seeing in my life! I had never seen so many people die—so many innocent victims on both sides died needlessly. I had never seen so many American soldiers, Blacks, Whites and Mexicans, die crawling in mud and blood, with brains hanging out, feet hanging off their bodies, fingers hanging off and eyes shot out. I had never seen men shot in their stomachs, in their hearts, chests and in their privates! I had never seen men with half of their faces blown off or half an arm blown off. No, I had never seen people suffer as much as what I witnessed in the Vietnam War.

I saw men shot in the mouth who lived in pain, holding their palates. I saw people get their tongues shot out and still live. I saw men who got shot in the chest and died and others who got shot in the chest and lived with a big hole in them. I saw some who got show in the eye and lived and some who got shot in an arm and died. I witnessed feet stumble over legs separated from bodies, heads, hearts, brains, eyes and unrecognizable pieces of the human body all lying on the ground. The sights that I saw were horrendous. There were times when I saw pieces of white and black flesh mixed, when I saw nappy heads mixed with straight hair heads and could tell that somebody black was involved and that the black and white persons had both been blown to smithereens.

Indeed, the Vietnam War was a tragic thing for me, and whenever I try to tell people and explain how tragic it was, I pretend not to look at them. I put my head down and catch a glimpse of them from the corner of my eye very sharply. I usually notice them nodding their heads up and down as a way of saying yes and that they are listening to me, but I also know that they will never grasp in their heads what actually went on over there because what happened over there is impossible to grasp unless a person has lived it.

EPILOGUE

I thank God above that I survived Vietnam, that I came back to the United States, but I did not come back completely whole. Vietnam took its toll on me, as it did so many other American men, and I came back with my own burdens to bear.

Luckily, I understand my sickness—Post Traumatic Syndrome/Panic Disorder/Agent Orange. I understand that my eyes took in more than my brain could stand and overloaded it, and this resulted in my severe stress. I understand that I got exposed to chemicals that were meant for the enemy. Yet, I am blessed, and I wish to give all my thanks to God that He has allowed me to write this book and give some true insights on what happened in Vietnam.

Still, all of the story is not told, and it will never be completely told because I just can't tell it all! However, the strange thing is that in my head I know it all! I can remember it all. I simply cannot tell it all!

Again, I want to give thanks to God up above for letting me live through that war, for letting me tell others about the war and now letting people read about it. I want everybody to know that it was God that enabled me to come back to the States physically whole. I say "thank you" to God for bringing me back in my right mind and with all of my limbs. Even though I am sick with a nervous condition, I am still wonderfully blessed.

To the readers, I just want to say that God is an Almighty God. I knew when I went to Vietnam that he was with me, but at that time I was not serving Him. I believed in Him; I knew that He existed, and I said my prayers at all times. Yet, I did not truly serve Him, doing the things He wanted me to do and doing them from my heart. Now that's different. I serve Him faithfully, and I can sincerely say, "God, I thank you for looking over me. Thank you for giving me the strength and ability to carry on, O Heavenly Lord. Thank you from your Holy Hills for looking after me."

Now, for those readers who may want to know what I think about this country after engaging in such a brutal war, my response is simple. This is my country! This is where I was born, and this is where I will die. Fighting for my country has been a double-edged sword for me, as it is for any black American. I say that because I went to Vietnam and fought a war over there, and I came back home, and I still have to fight a war in these United States of American—a war against ignorance and racial prejudice.

Whenever the government tells a person that he has to go over and fight in a foreign country, supposedly for the rights of others and then that person has to come home and fight for his own basic human and civil rights, than any deaf, dumb or blind person can see that, that isn't right. So I ask the United States to get it right! We cannot send people to other countries to fight and try to police this whole world when we don't have our business together right here on our own soil!

In case there is any doubt, I am talking about the relationship between blacks and whites. We are as separated as the Pacific and the Atlantic Ocean, and in between, there is a lot of evil that is lurking in both races. We must start praying for each other—blacks and whites, men and women, girls and boys—because there will come a day, and I truly believe, when we are going to need each other. As I tried to communicate time and time again, during the war, when the bullets started flying, race ran! I repeat! When the bullets started flying, color—the negative thinking in the mind about color—ran! We started helping each other; we forgot about who was black, white or Mexican. We had to fight together side by side, and I am convinced that we are going to need each other again before everything is over here on this earth. Thus, it's important that we all pray for this country. After all, this is our country, and, indeed, this is my country!

CPSIA information can be obtained
at www.ICGtesting.com
Printed in the USA
LVHW042208161221
706396LV00012B/1840